After the Sundown

After the Sundown

by Pat Jordan

DODD, MEAD & COMPANY
New York

1   2   3   4   5   6   7   8   9   10

Library of Congress Cataloging in Publication Data

Jordan, Pat.
  After the sundown.

    1. Athletes—United States—Biography. 2. Athletes—
United States—Retirement. I. Title.
GV697.A1J67   796'.092'2   [B]   79-9533
ISBN 0-396-07773-0

For Peter, thanks

Contents

Foreword

Every athlete, at some point in his life, must make his peace with his sport. There comes a time when he can no longer play successfully the game that has sustained him. For some this moment comes early in a career. A debilitating injury may occur while the athlete is in his teens or he may face the sudden realization that he lacks the talent to go on. Others may move to a more advanced level of play—college or even the professional ranks—before, finally, their talent betrays them. But no athlete, not even a superstar, can play his sport forever. Athletes in all sports have one thing in common: sooner or later they all must retire.

This book is a collection of profiles of athletes who have had to leave their sport. Some, like Phil Hill, the world champion race car driver, left at the height of their powers and found successful careers outside their sport. Others, such as Jim Bouton and Jerome Evans, had more modest careers that they used as springboards to other pursuits tangentially tied to their playing days. And still others, like Art Heyman, Bo Belinsky, and Richie Connors, were forced to quit before they fulfilled their talent and have yet to make their peace with the loss of sport from their lives.

Yet once all these men, both the successful and the less successful, retired from their sport, they were forced to reexamine the way they and others saw them. Because they were no longer athletes, they had lost that indefinable resource—the athlete's glow—which can be dimmed only when one ceases to participate. This resource, the inheritance of fame or talent, may be real or illusory. In the eyes of the nonathlete, however, it does exist. The athlete is different. He is privy to certain mysteries that elevate him from the common herd. He is blessed in a world of the unblessed. In his book, *The Summer Game,* Roger Angell writes, "we (nonathletes) had never made it. We would never know the rich joke that doubled over three young pitchers in front of the dugout; we would never be part of that golden company on the field, which each of us, certainly for one moment of his life, had wanted more than anything else in the world to join."

Whether those rookies said anything of substance or humor is irrelevant. Whether there was any mystery in Hank Aaron, other than his being blessed with incredibly quick wrists, is also irrelevant. It matters only that nonathletes believe an athlete is special and so bestow on him a homage that brings with it a host of privileges. For a player certain rules are suspended, amenities not required, life's unpleasantness diminished, and his every deficiency muted in the eyes of the unblessed. In a player's presence, the conversation invariably revolves around him, his talent, and his sport. Even far removed from his playing field, he remains the hub of a private universe that is satisfyingly simple. Athletes float above the complex and the disagreeable, which become for them the unreal. An athlete's world is transformed into the "real" world.

The loss of this privilege at the end of a career can be traumatic, and an athlete fears it more even than the loss of his talent or fame or salary. Once he can no longer trade on the resource that defined him, he must seek a new definition. An athlete who leaves his sport early enough will have time to redefine himself, to grow outside sport. But one who retires late in life does not. He is so rooted to his sport and its privileges that their loss causes great frustration. These athletes—the most successful ones whose careers span the greatest number of years—confront the most devastating readjustment to the real world. They must ask themselves, like that young pitcher in *A False Spring*, "What would I be without baseball? I could think of nothing." For many, there is no longer enough time to find an answer.

After the Sundown

After the Sundown

It is 1 P.M. Football Coach Tom (Bull) Bulwith stands with his players and their mascot, a small goat that is urinating on the stage in the William L. Dickinson High School auditorium. Eight hundred students are screeching, chanting, cheering, stamping, and otherwise exhorting their team to victory in tomorrow's game. Bulwith, a veteran coach in his first year at Dickinson, had not expected such a rally at this soot-stained, brick-Gothic school whose students ordinarily drowse in class and litter the graffitied halls with milk cartons, candy wrappers, and cigarette butts. Dickinson, located close by the turnpike in the smog of Jersey City, has difficulty rousing its students for any endeavor, especially football, since the team has not won a game in five years.

The cheering, however, seems off-center. It is not directed toward Coach Bulwith, who is shouting into a microphone at center stage, but to the right and below, at the foot of the stage where Jim Bouton, the former New York Yankee and now CBS-TV sportscaster, is aiming a microphone at the chanting students while a camera crew films them. The students, as if on cue, rise from their seats and surge toward Bouton. On stage Bulwith turns slightly and tries to follow them with his voice. Bouton is swept up in the pandemonium. "Jeez, look at 'em!" he shouts. "Imagine being sixteen again! I'd give $10,000 cash to be tomorrow's quarterback!" The chanting students surround him, press him back against a wall, and he disappears from view. Meanwhile, Bulwith has made a 90-degree turn and is shouting exhortations at the backs of the students.

3 P.M.—Driving back to the CBS building in Manhattan, Bouton says, "Any good reporter twists reality. He alters it just by the way he sees it. In my case, I alter it twice: once by the way I see it, and a second time just by my presence. My being there with a camera affected the way those kids acted. Who's to say how. You never know. Partly, it's just the camera and partly it's my being there, rather than my reason for being there. I ask them how it feels to lose 43 games in a row, and they ask me for my autograph. All they are thinking is, 'Hey, man, I'm talking to Jim Bouton!' It's nice being recognized, but I feel I would be anyway. It makes my job more fun but it doesn't help me do a good job. It would have made a better story if I could have gotten those kids to

sing the school fight song. But all they wanted to do was cheer."

5 P.M.—Bouton, shirtless, bends forward, sticking his head into a sink. He turns on the water and begins shampooing his hair. Beside him in the cramped CBS men's room, Ron Swoboda, also an ex-Yankee and now a sportscaster, lathers his face with shaving cream, leans toward a mirror, and begins to shave.

"We are doing our toilette," says Bouton from the sink bowl.

Swoboda, examining one half of his shaved face, says, "That's right, Jim. We always do our toilette before we go on the air."

"No kidding," says Bouton. "It's a tough habit to break. As a ballplayer you always took a shower and shaved as soon as you got to the clubhouse for a night game. It made you feel good, freshened you up so that you felt like you were starting the day all over again. It was a shock to discover that people in the real world didn't do that. They showered in the morning and that was it."

Bouton and Swoboda take great pains with their afternoon toilette partly because they are not as sure of themselves in their present profession as they were in their former ("Would you believe," says Bouton, "that we get more letters commenting on how we look on TV than what we say?") and also because it is a link with the clubhouse camaraderie of the past.

Bouton lifts his wet head from the sink, rubs his hair with a towel and says, "Can I borrow your drier, Ron?"

"Sure you can," says Swoboda, and he hands over a woman's hair drier.

"You know how it is, Ron," says Bouton, fingering strands of damp hair. "I can't do a thing with it. Those frizzies."

"Yes, Jim, I know just what you mean. The ends split. The technique is to dry them while you're combing."

"You better believe it, Ron. That's the great thing about this ConAir, Pro Style hair drier. It lets you dry your hair without blowing it all over your face." Bouton bends over so that his hair falls toward the floor, then turns on the blower. Through the noise, he says, "Can you imagine a ballplayer from the '30s walking into to-day's clubhouse? All those guys with their hair driers. Jeez, I'd love to see that."

When his hair is dry and he has taken pains to see that it looks properly rumpled (a few quick tosses of the head until it falls in place), Bouton says, "Seriously though, this is the kind of thing I miss most. Locker-room humor. I used to love the bawdy way of ballplayers. You never find that gross humor in the real world. Around here, if you have a complexion problem nobody mentions it. In the locker room they call you 'pizza face.' That may be cruel, but it's an open, refresh-ing honesty, the kind of thing you'd expect among young kids. Maybe that's why I loved sports. They pro-vided an extended childhood. Everyone else was wearing a suit and tie and you could still be a child. There were other things too. Special privileges. My bags were carried, my room arranged, my uniform hung in the locker, a special parking sticker always on my car. Everything was arranged. You flowed through the system with all the little annoyances eliminated. A place was made for you at the head of the line. Now I have to make my own reservations, carry my own bags—little things, really, but a constant reminder of what I no longer am. It's a hard reality to face. Jeez, I used to love waking up in the morning. It was great to get out of bed knowing you were a big-league ballplayer. It was fun to walk down the street. You felt good, physically and mentally, and never seemed to get colds like other people. You felt you could knock down walls. Of course, I never thought baseball was an important thing. But I was lucky to be doing it. A guy I played with says I was a fan who got to pitch in the big leagues. Willie Mays wasn't a fellow player to me, he was the Say Hey Kid.

"It was like getting on a bus heading for Oregon and getting sidetracked in Las Vegas. You only have a dime in your pocket so you figure, what the hell, throw it in a slot machine and pull the lever. A whole load of dimes comes out, so you go to the roulette table and you win there, and before the day is over you've got all this money, someone else's money. Know what I mean? You wake up and say, 'What am I doing here?'

"There were disadvantages. I hated the travel, being

away from my wife and kids half the year. But there was even something good about that. The time I did spend at home was richer, the hours with the kids more important. Now I see them all the time and things are not the same. As a ballplayer everything was richer. You had more extreme ups and downs but that just made the taste buds work better."

Bouton puts on his shirt, his tie, and then a black velvet sport jacket. He studies himself in the mirror, narrows his already narrow eyes and leaves the room.

Walking through the CBS studio, he says, "If I had a chance to be a big-leaguer tomorrow, I'd leave this job in a minute. When I was on the way out with the Astros—just before *Ball Four* was published—ABC-TV offered me a job for twice the money I was making. The network said I'd have to leave the Astros immediately. I said, 'Are you kidding? Leave the Houston Astros just to be on television?' I finally took the job when the Astros shipped me back to the minors.

"I was terrified when I left baseball, a fish out of water. I still won't admit my career's over. I know the date and the hour, but my mind refuses to accept the fact that I couldn't go back if I tried. I'm only thirty-six. Sometimes I'm pitching in this semi-pro league in New Jersey and for an inning or two I can feel it all coming back. After the game you say to yourself, 'I've got it again! If I work a little bit for the next few weeks I can get it all together. I'll get back there!' And the cruel thing is, the minute you start thinking that way, it's gone. The next game you're warming up and it's not there. You say to yourself, 'No, that's not it. Be patient, it'll come.' It isn't there after the first inning so you start the second, saying, 'No, you don't quite have it, but don't panic, there's still time.' And you go through the whole game and the touch never comes back. So for the next few games you forget about it, and then about a month later it comes back again for an inning or two. You start all over. It's like an evil elf tempting you."

6:30 P.M.—Bouton is sitting in a barber chair in a brilliantly lighted room and scrutinizing his image in a huge mirror. Also reflected in the mirror is a Formica counter littered with soiled tissues, artists' brushes, pencils, pastel crayons, jars of pancake make-up. Standing beside Bouton is a short, heavyset woman with a smooth, pink, baby face that is perfectly made-up. While Bouton watches, she pencils in his eyebrows and carries on a conversation with a gray-haired woman seated on the other side of Bouton and absorbed in her knitting.

The woman with the baby face puts down her pencil and stares at Bouton's reflection. Satisfied, she picks up an artist's brush, daubs it with make-up, and begins covering Bouton's forehead, the hollows of his cheeks, and under his chin. His face grows orange as she works. He watches her carefully, and when she finally puts down the brush they examine the result. His face has lost all its tone and is a solid, deep orange. There is no hint of beard. He moves his head slightly, left, then right and, finally satisfied, gets out of the chair.

"It's the camera," says the make-up lady. "It distorts reality, adding 20 pounds to a person's appearance. You need make-up to distort the person's face in such a way that when he gets in front of the camera the face appears the way it would in reality. By distorting it with make-up, it looks natural."

6:40 P.M.—Rolland Smith, Dave Marash, Ron Swoboda, and Pat Collins, members of the CBS-TV news staff, are sitting behind a long, irregular desk under bright conical lights in the studio that serves as the Channel 2 early evening news set. They read from a script or smile straight ahead while, in the shadows, television cameras roll forward for close-ups, pause, and then retreat into the shadows as other cameras advance. In the darkness behind the cameras Bouton is waiting for the cue to replace Swoboda on the set so that he can deliver his news feature on Dickinson High School and its losing streak. Bouton, fidgeting with his tie, says in a hushed voice, "There's a great similarity between being on television and pitching before thousands of people. In both cases you're working under pressure, you have to be able to concentrate, to be able to focus on one thought quickly, and then just as quickly stand off from it. It helps to be a little tense. Most guys try to eliminate that tenseness before they face the cameras. I like butterflies in my stomach. When I was pitching I tried to manufacture butterflies. I used them to get a better pitch out of myself. I still do."

While Bouton is talking, Marash is delivering a news bulletin on recent developments in the case of Hurricane Carter, a black boxer serving a life term for murdering three men in New Jersey. Two witnesses to the murders seven years before have just come forth to say they lied at Carter's trial, when they swore they had seen him at the scene of the crime. Marash finishes, and there is a pause on the set for a commercial. Bouton slips into Swoboda's seat, shuffles through his papers and prepares to deliver his story.

7 P.M.—Just as he is about to leave the CBS building for supper, Bouton receives a telephone call from a woman chastising him for making a fool out of the winless high school football players. Bouton tries to explain that he wasn't trying to make a fool of anyone, that he really does hope the team wins its game tomorrow. The woman says something. Bouton replies and slams down the receiver. The call has upset him. "How could anyone take offense at that story?" he says. "It was just a funny story."

Bouton treats everything he talks about on television in a humorous vein. Even when he is being sharply critical of, say, the baseball Establishment, he strives for humor. This is his nature. Often he hits his mark. But when he does not, the result is strained. He is a natural entertainer, inclined to deal with the quick, the light, the superficial. He says, "I could have put in for the Hurricane Carter story, but decided not to. I took the Dickinson kids instead." He shakes his head. "That Carter story, I don't know. The magnitude of it scared me."

8 P.M.—Two attractive women in their twenties enter the restaurant—a dark, paneled, sawdusty pub with an Irish name that gives it the license to charge $2.50 for a hamburger. They notice Bouton eating supper and move to the empty table beside him. Without glancing up, he smiles and says, "Things are going to go downhill from here." Then he returns to the subject of conversation. "The television job just fell in my lap. It scares me to think what I'd be doing if it hadn't. I like TV now. It has a lot of the advantages baseball had, pays a nice salary, and there is the recognition factor. When people keep asking for your autograph you don't feel you've lost it. I can have an impact. There are millions of people out there whom I can make see things through my eyes. Sometimes, though, you feel helpless. You wonder, do they really care what you think or say, or is it just that they're curious because you're a celebrity? Once you become a public personality everybody wants to use you for some cause or other. If I was rich I'd give them my money; if I was a nobody I'd give my time. Because I'm a celebrity I give them my face. You wonder too, *should* they pay attention to you?

"I'm trying to show people that sports are fun, that

the guy playing touch football in Central Park or the Dickinson team trying to break a losing streak is as important as the professionals. People should play sports more and watch less. I really loved to play baseball. When I wrote my book I wasn't trying to knock the game, just trying to show people how much fun the sport was. It upset me to go on a television talk show where they would sit me down with Dave Meggyesy. He would be wearing his New Left hippie costume and talking about the evils of football and society, and I'd wonder what the hell I was doing there. If I had my way right now I'd go back to the locker room. I might not fit in anymore, but I'd still like to do it."

Throughout the conversation the girls have been casting glances at Bouton. There is something about him that is strange, unreal. It is his face, waxy and orange. He has not removed his make-up and here in the restaurant, away from the distortions of the television camera, he looks unnatural.

"I live from month to month, doing whatever seems interesting at the moment," Bouton is saying. "Sometimes I wish I could do something anonymously. You know, like working with wood. I love the smell of freshly cut wood. I'd love to go off with my family someplace and just make things. But I don't think I could. Everyone would think I was crazy. If I really did go to the country, I might go crazy. Working with wood sounds nice, but maybe it would smell rotten after a while. Jeez, waking up every morning seeing that same wood. I'd have to enter something in a contest. I'd have to win a prize. And when I did, everything would change."

●

In the back seat of a taxi moving through New York traffic, Arthur Bruce Heyman, a balding, thirty-two-year-old businessman, is silent. His face is blank. His mouth is open, long jaw dropping as if unhinged, eyes wincing as if with pain as he tries to focus on a half-remembered moment in his life, a moment once filled with intensity but grown hazy with the passage of time during a life now devoid of intensity. He leans forward and hugs himself. His knees are jacked up in a fetal position, and slowly, rhythmically, he begins to rock, back and forth, back and forth.

In 1963 Art Heyman, a 6′5″ senior at Duke University, was voted the college basketball Player of the Year by the Associated Press, *The Sporting News,* and the Atlantic Coast Conference. During his three varsity seasons he led his team to national rankings (10th in '61, 10th in '62, second in '63). Heyman was a three-time All-America and captain of the Duke team in his final year. "I put the school on the map. I was the first guy who ever went to Duke," he says, ignoring—or oblivious of—the athletic contributions of men like Ace Parker, Sonny Jurgensen, and Dave Sime.

The product of affluent parents, Heyman grew up on

Long Island in an area where everyone his age wanted to own a car, while he wanted only to play basketball. "I had to play by myself," he says, "so I would go to Manhattan Beach in Brooklyn where guys like Connie Hawkins and Tony Jackson hung around. There were about ten of us, and I was one of those who didn't get caught in the fixing scandals a few years later. The fixers never approached me because I was too affluent. They figured I didn't need the money."

Heyman graduated from high school with superior grades and nearly one hundred offers for college scholarships. One morning Adolph Rupp appeared on his doorstep. Rupp told Heyman's mother that her son should go to the best basketball school in the country, where he would be coached by the best basketball coach in the country. Mrs. Heyman, smiling, said, "Really, Mr. Rupp. And where's that?"

"He was speechless," says Heyman. "At the time I could have gone to any basketball school I wanted. But I was on an ego trip. I wanted to prove that even without basketball I could get into the toughest schools. I'd already had offers from Yale and Harvard, which knew about me, so I applied to one of the few schools that hadn't offered me a scholarship, Williams College in Massachusetts. I applied like any other student. I was going to pay my way if Williams would just take me as a student. But the school turned me down. When I told a friend what had happened he called the Williams coach and told him the university had just turned down the best high school basketball player in the country. The coach went out of his mind. The next day I got a call from Williams. They told me my application had been reevaluated and I had been accepted after all. I told them to go to hell."

As in many of the stories Heyman recounts about his career, the latter may be an exaggeration, if not a downright fabrication; these days officials at Williams College deny it. Recalling his more glorious past, Heyman remembers things as they should have been for a man of greatness.

He enrolled at Duke in the fall of 1959 because the basketball team was only fair and it appealed to his vanity to imagine that he could singlehandedly reverse its fortunes. He had a genuine affection for the new head coach, Vic Bubas, whom he describes as being "like a father." Heyman needed a father, for it soon became obvious that his talent for basketball was exceeded only by his talent for troublemaking. He was involved in numerous fights both on and off the court, one of which (a fraternity-house scuffle in which he allegedly struck a pre-med student causing him eye damage) resulted in Heyman's unsuccessfully being sued for $85,000. On another occasion he was accused of assaulting a North Carolina University male cheerleader at halftime. The charges were dismissed.

On still another occasion he claims he absconded with a nineteen-year-old Duke coed, crossed into South Carolina and checked into a motel for the weekend. He signed the motel register Mr. and Mrs. Oscar Robertson. ("Oscar was always my hero," he says.) The clerk knew that Heyman, a white man with a New York City accent, was not the Big O, so he promptly called the state police, who arrested Heyman and charged him with violating the Mann Act. In jail, he was allowed one phone call. "I called Bubas," he says today. "He phoned the Duke president, and he called the governor of North Carolina, who called the lieutenant governor of South Carolina. That man got me out of jail and flew me back to Duke in his private plane." Again, the principals deny the entire story.

"I was the biggest thing that ever happened to Duke," says Heyman. "At that time it was a Methodist school that hadn't integrated, and I, a Jew, was the star of the team. Of course, not too many people knew I was a Jew. They thought I was a Wasp from Connecticut. Those Southerners couldn't comprehend a Jew being a great athlete. I was always getting letters of praise from organizations like The Fellowship of Christian Athletes, and a man in Tuscaloosa named Shelton used to regularly exhort me to keep upholding the principles of white Christian supremacy. Once he offered me a membership in the Ku Klux Klan. He was the head of the Klan. Man, I really loved Duke. I was a hero."

Once Heyman left the university he never was a hero again. He did, however, continue to play basketball. He was the No. 1 draft choice of the New York Knicks and received a sizable bonus. He played with the Knicks for two years without cracking the regular starting lineup, and in 1965 was claimed on waivers by the San Francisco Warriors. All told, Art Heyman played six seasons of professional basketball with seven different teams in the NBA and ABA. At times during those years he was a good basketball player, but more often he was merely a journeyman.

Not surprisingly, he takes little delight in recalling his professional days. "I never did live up to my God-given potential," he says. "It's the one thing I feel bad about." The reasons for this failure, he claims, are varied, although he refuses to admit that his talents simply paled in comparison to those of players like Jerry West and Oscar Robertson. Heyman blames his failure on a chronic bad back and the fact that "I couldn't adjust to the cold professional attitude. It was a head thing with me. When I first came into the NBA I was dedicated, but the other pros didn't care. They would go through the motions all season and only try hard in the playoffs. During the season they only hustled the last five minutes of a game so they could make the point spread. Without gambling nobody would watch a pro game.

"I remember one night against the Royals in Madison Square Garden. We were losing by 30 points with five minutes to go, and nobody would leave. The fans were waiting to see if the Royals would make the spread, which was 22 points. We cut their lead to 21 with five seconds left and the fans were going wild. Finally Jerry Lucas [then with the Royals] hit a 30-foot shot at the buzzer to boost the Royals over the spread, and the fans ran onto the court and carried Lucas off on their shoulders. I couldn't adjust to that. In the pros everybody's out for himself. Guys like Wilt Chamberlain would push away little kids asking for autographs. Man, those guys should thank God for what they got. Instead, they're making $300,000 a year and bitching about the long season, how tired they are, how they have to wake up at nine o'clock in the morning for a team meeting, and here's some poor guy stuck on the thruway every morning at seven o'clock trying to get to the city. I'd like to see those jocks go out into the real world instead of living in that fantasy world. Man, I thank God I had a brain so I could make it outside of basketball.

"I was twenty-eight when I quit. I could still be playing, but I was disenchanted, wanted to do something else with my life. I loved basketball. In college, if I let my team down I couldn't sleep. I would have been the greatest basketball player ever if only I could have found that college atmosphere in the pros."

Heyman retired from professional basketball in 1970, playing his last game with the Pittsburgh Pipers. He had been told he would need a spinal fusion if he were to continue. His back still causes him such pain that the slightest unexpected movement makes him grimace. He walks with his shoulders hunched, his arms pressed tightly to his sides, his legs stiff and unbending. He can take only the tiniest steps, as if shackles bind his ankles, and each painful stride jerks his shoulders left, then right. The walk was made famous by Charlie Chaplin, only Heyman's is even more restricted than Chaplin's, and Heyman is so much taller, a towering man, a trussed Gulliver in a world of Lilliputians. Heyman takes whirlpool treatments and almost daily massages at Opus, the combination restaurant/discotheque/health club he recently opened on New York's East Side. He cannot avail himself of the club's exercise room, paddleball court, or billiard table because of his back.

Opus is unimpressive on the outside, with a drab concrete facade and a pennant proclaiming its name, but the interior is plushly decorated in a style best described as Bordello Gothic—crushed red velvet and mahogany. It is only one of the many business investments Heyman has made with the bonus he received from the Knicks before his rookie season. During his playing years he invested wisely in Southern real estate and New York City discotheques so that today he is relatively wealthy, leading an entrepreneur's life—waking at noon, lunching at his restaurant, checking menus, counting the house, greeting people, sitting for long hours in a booth off the dining room, waiting for the last of his patrons to leave before closing up and returning to his apartment at dawn.

Heyman was sitting in the Opus bar one recent midnight, waiting anxiously while Bob Arum, the promoter of Evel Knievel's Snake River Canyon jump, dined with friends. Whenever Arum's waitress passed, Heyman whispered in her ear, listened to her reply, and nodded.

Sitting across from Heyman and looking equally anxious were his business associates in Opus, Joel Korby and Dr. Arthur Weider. Weider was wearing a white plantation suit and smoking a cigarette in a long holder. Korby, attired in crushed velvet, resembled a twitchy Joel Grey. Beside Heyman sat his girl friend of the moment, a thin, plain girl with a Brooklyn accent. She had only known him a few weeks but found him not at all what she expected. "I'd heard he was such a wild man," she said. "But he's nothing like that."

"No one would think I ever was an athlete," Heyman said that night. "I don't even think of myself as an athlete. I don't feel like one anymore and shy away from jocks and people who knew me then. I'm a businessman. I would feel like an intruder in that jock world. You are forgotten quickly."

Bob Arum appeared, looking for the men's room. Heyman motioned to him and asked about Knievel's jump. After some small talk in which Arum complimented Heyman on the decor of the restaurant ("Very classy, Art, very classy") and wished him luck, Heyman could restrain himself no longer. "Bob, how was your steak?"

Arum paused a deliberate beat, and then said, "It was very good, Art, really good."

"No, tell me the truth. How was it?"

Arum nodded. "It was O.K. Not bad."

Korby blurted out, "We got to know, Bob. It's important to us."

Arum threw up his hands. "Well, actually, it could have been better."

"Thanks, Bob," says Korby. "That's the kind of thing we got to know, else how are we going to improve?"

"Actually, it could have been a lot better," added Arum. "It wasn't too good at all."

Shortly after midnight Heyman and his girl friend left Opus for the short taxi ride to his other East Side restaurant, the Gobblers Knob, a less flamboyantly decorated singles bar managed by Heyman's ex-wife Barbara. "We're on very good terms," he said.

Barbara Heyman is a striking strawberry blonde with huge eyes, an upturned nose, and moist, pouty lips. She bears a close resemblance to Xavier Cugat's discovery, Charo. Like Charo, she too has a soft, full figure, although there is nothing of the dumb blonde about her. She was born and raised in Texas, has lived in New York City for seven years and now possesses that typically New York wariness about things and people that tends to give her soft physical appearance a sharp edge. She met Heyman when he was with the Pipers. Then, he had the confidence only an athlete can have, knowing his every deficiency, personal or physical, would be masked by an inexhaustible resource, the drawing account of his fame.

"Art is a very intelligent man," his ex-wife said. "He is the kind of man who could fall out of an airplane and land on his feet. We are good friends, even after the divorce. I don't know if I should mention this but, well, you see how he's getting bald. He's so conscious that he's losing his hair that whenever he has a big date with a new girl he comes over to my place and makes me set and wrap his hair, and then comb it over his bald spot."

January 1975

The Man Who Was Cut Out for the Job

Jerome Evans is forty, with skin the color of milk chocolate. His weight has not varied a pound in twenty years. His body is so lean and tight that his muscles, veins, and bones are visible as distinct elements through the thin cloth of his skin. His body is so taut that it seems to have no potential to give but only to rip.

Evans is constantly aware of the condition of his body, his clothes, the way he walks, talks, and eats, all his natural mannerisms because, as he says, "Everyone's looking at me." As a black man operating in a white world, Evans realizes eyes are turned on him, and so he has turned his own eyes inward to insure that nothing of Jerome Evans is visible to others that is not first visible to himself. To Evans the most reprehensible weakness would be for some trait or mannerism to slip out without his consent. Though he is constantly and consciously

23

sifting possibilities and deciding what to reveal or conceal, Evans' selections are not based on any desire to deceive. Rather, he wants to create the self he thinks he should be. All his life he has been confronted by two cultures: black and white. And when they are in contradiction, he has not always been sure which to choose. If Evans were a romantic he would simply choose that which is most natural to him rather than that which is foreign. But what is natural and what is best in a given society are not necessarily the same. Because of his wish to pick and choose the best from each culture, Evans' life is a precarious balancing act. He never seems to relax. Every decision, no matter how insignificant, must be debated thoroughly before being acted on. For instance, when a white football player on the Williams team scores a touchdown and Evans is about to congratulate the boy, one can almost hear the whirrings in the coach's mind. He raises his arm to put it on the boy's shoulder, the arm suspended in midair, and then lets it fall to his side as he rejects that possibility and instead shakes the player's hand.

"I've built up in my mind what a man should be," he says. "This ability not to let down in front of people, whether they're black or white, is part of it. Some things I may want to do, but I won't. If I get drunk once in a while, lots of blacks will take comfort from that because it will prove I'm no better than them, and whites will take comfort too, because it'll prove I'm just 'like every other nigger.' But I won't be just any other nigger. I'm a man like anybody else."

If the black community in Burlington has any complaint about Evans, it is that he is too much his own man. He is too aloof and so, in a way, inaccessible to their pressures. He does not view problems externally. His solutions are arrived at in relation to himself, his wife, and his two young children, and not in relation to "his people." He has said many times, "I don't trust leaders of 'people.' You have to beware of saints—they're dangerous. I want only to lead myself and my family."

On his graduation from North Carolina Central University in 1955, Evans decided to coach at primarily black schools throughout North Carolina. He had no desire to penetrate the white world. However, after moving from one black high school to another, year after year as the tide of integration rolled through the state, Evans began to see himself as a prehistoric mammal fleeing evolution and faced with extinction. Soon he would have to quit coaching, for there would be no black schools left to hire him. However, quite another choice—and a surprising one—presented itself in 1970 when he was asked to take the job at Williams High. He decided to accept the position and with it the pressures of integration.

Before the Burlington school board offered that position, however, it had had to oust C. A. Frye. A decade before, Frye's teams had been among the most powerful in North Carolina, but as other schools accepted integration, and with it large numbers of swift, elusive black football players, Williams remained a bastion of white supremacy. Its teams began to win less frequently, and the fortunes of their fiery coach declined accordingly. During these years Jerome Evans was molding well-disciplined black teams at Jordan Sellers that posted such records as 7–2 and 8–1, while Frye's players were struggling through seasons of 3–6–1 and 2–8.

Even so, Frye remained feared and respected as the Williams coach. His violent outbursts toward players were legendary among the townspeople, half of whom thought them a disgrace while the other half reveled in their ferociousness. He was known to tear the shirts off the backs of players and swear with such vehemence that the school's cheerleaders would run for shelter.

"There were times if I had a knife I would have killed Coach Frye," said Mike Pierce, a white player. "He had no patience with anyone. When I was on the junior varsity I could hear him yelling from the other field and I was scared at the thought of ever playing for such a man. But one day in school he called me Mike and said how the team would need me the following year, and after that I was crazy about him. He screamed and cussed all right, and when you stunk he made a little raspberry sound and did a war dance around you like you were burning at the stake. He made you want to quit football and just grow your hair. And a lot of boys did quit, but maybe Frye gave them an excuse to do what they wanted. He brought out a lot of things in you that you never knew existed—both the best and the worst." Frye might have retained his coaching job indefinitely had it not been for a number of incidents, a few of which he was involved in, but some of which he took no part in whatsoever. Like Jerome Evans, he too was a victim of the times.

One night as he was about to go to bed, he heard a commotion on his front lawn. Since he lived in a section of Burlington that was being encroached upon by the Negro population, Frye immediately assumed it was a "nigger prowler." He grabbed his gun, flung open the door, and fired at the first thing that moved. He discovered that he had "winged" a white boy who had come to the house to see his pretty daughter, Cathy. The incident did not sit well with members of the school board, who noted that he could have handled the situation in "a less volatile way." A short while later, Frye was taken to court by a youth who claimed the coach had punched him on discovering him in the school gym at an hour when it was supposed to be closed. Frye was eventually exonerated, but a few months afterward he was rumored to have pushed another boy down a flight of stairs at Williams in a fit of anger. It was said that the boy was paralyzed for life and that the police were hunting Frye. The rumors were simply untrue, but it no longer really mattered. Many of the city's residents felt they had had enough of C. A. Frye.

"The point was," said Craig White, a recent Williams

graduate, that "everyone believed those rumors about
Frye. That was the kind of man he was. There were
vestiges of fanaticism about him. When he played basketball he took more pleasure in knocking you over
than in going around you. But still, I was fascinated by
him. You had to accept him for what he was because if
you thought about it, that would ruin him for you."

Frye could not be removed without sufficient cause,
but school officials found that. In the spring of 1969,
black citizens in Burlington rioted and a good deal of
their anger was over the fact that Williams High would
not have a single black cheerleader during the following
football season. Later the same year a black citizens'
committee demanded that on the full integration of Williams a black head coach should be appointed for one of
the school's three major sports. The superintendent of
schools, Dr. Brank Proffitt, saw in this demand an op-
portunity not only to satisfy the town's 8000 blacks, but
also the whites clamoring for Frye's dismissal. Early in
1970 Proffitt called Frye to his office and informed him
that he was being elevated to the administrative position
of athletic director of the Burlington senior high
schools. Frye accepted Proffitt's offer, but privately he
remained determined to fight what amounted to his
dismissal as Williams football coach.

The school superintendent was relieved. He felt the
success or failure of the integration of the Williams team
would directly affect the mood of the town. "And I
decided we needed a black man as coach," said Dr. Pro-

ffitt. "One who was controlled and disciplined. Jerome Evans was constructive and not bitchin' about the past sins of whites. He had a sense of what the long haul was. Although Frye believed he was a just man, I knew justice wasn't only a matter of black and white. There was a lot of gray in it, and Frye never could see gray in any situation. He was too simplistic."

When news hit Burlington that Frye had been removed as coach, a number of his supporters threatened to call a town meeting to get him reinstated. Two hundred white students walked out of classes at Williams in support of Frye. They were led by a number of football players. After several tense hours, during which the blacks threatened a counterdemonstration, the situation was resolved. Frye called off his supporters on being warned by Dr. Proffitt that if Burlington had another riot his credibility as a coach would be seriously jeopardized throughout the state.

The football players returned meekly to classes the following day and Frye dropped out of sight until midsummer, when it was announced he had accepted the post of football coach and athletic director at small Gibsonville High School, only 10 miles west of Burlington. "I wish he had gone to Florida as he threatened," said Dr. Proffitt, "rather than hanging like a shadow over the town and Jerome Evans."

When Evans started football practice in late August, he did not have to prove anything to the black players

who had known him at Sellers and would now be playing for Williams. His challenge lay with the team's
whites. "I worried about how I should treat those boys
who had supported Frye," said Evans. "Then I decided
to make believe nothing had happened and treat
everyone fair. I wasn't very forceful at first because I
didn't want to scare anyone off. The whites had to be
shown that all the things they'd been brought up to
believe about blacks were false. And to build their confidence in me, and my own in myself, I had to show
them a black coach could win games. The Williams 4-A
conference was supposedly a lot tougher than the 3-A
conference that Sellers had played in, but I found it
wasn't. After we won a few games I could afford to get
tougher with some of the white boys."

Evans' white players and white assistant coaches
began accepting him, at least superficially. They did not
see, however, that his fairness was tipped in their favor,
since he showed more tolerance for the failures of white
players than he did for those of the blacks, many of
whom thought the coach was "a man possessed this
year."

"When Evans first came to Williams," said Mike
Pierce, "I thought he wouldn't even look at guys like me
who had walked out in support of Frye. But the first
time I met him he gave me a big smile and shook my
hand and told me he was relying on me, and after that I
knocked myself out liking him. All us whites did. But it
wasn't real. We were always wondering when we'd get

shafted for one of his blacks. Soon it occurred to us that maybe we wouldn't. If Evans had been an emotional type of guy, like Frye, we never would have relaxed. Another problem was that it was always there in the back of our minds that maybe Evans wasn't as good a coach as Frye. We never admitted it, probably not even to ourselves, but maybe it was because he was a black man. After we won a few games we accepted him more. I guess it's a shame that before we did, he had to prove he could win in this conference. If he was white he would have been accepted first, but because he's black he's accepted only for what he does, not for what he is."

Pierce and other whites were surprised by the cool way Evans handled situations that would have had Frye's neck deep red. One day while Evans was giving orders to his offensive team, a white player, William Whitley, was staring off into space.

"If Frye caught anyone daydreaming like that," said Pierce, "the guy would still be picking Frye's cleats out of his mouth. But Evans just gave Whitley that pained smile of his and said, 'William Whitley, whatever am I gonna do with you, boy?' I guess Whitley wouldn't even be on the team if Frye was coaching. Frye had no patience for dreamers, quitters, or anyone, really. If Frye doesn't like someone they don't exist anymore so far as he's concerned. Evans is the opposite. He's very decent to people he doesn't like, maybe even more decent than to people he does like."

But Evans was less than successful with two players.

One was a black halfback from Jordan Sellers, Larry Matkins; the other was the team's white quarterback, Fred Long, who had been one of Frye's stars. There is a picture of Larry Matkins in the 1969 Jordan Sellers yearbook. It shows a lean, intense black youth with a completely shaven head sweeping by the outstretched arms of a would-be tackler. As a 5' 10", 175-pound sophomore, Matkins was considered one of the best prospects in the South. It was reported that the University of Alabama was interested in him. He was fifteen years old. In 1970 he was elected a Williams co-captain, along with a white player, David Coleman, and he was expected to carry the team. But Matkins was to have a mediocre year. He was Evans' biggest disappointment. The coach said of him: "I see so much of myself in that boy, and I want him to excel so bad it hurts." To bring out the best in Matkins, Evans was unmerciful with him in practice. If Matkins gained 20 yards on a run, Evans berated him for not gaining 30. Many whites felt Evans was expecting too much of the boy, who was now competing against more efficient defenses than he had at Sellers. Evans could not see this. He said: "Matkins' difficulty, among other things, is that girl of his."

The girl was a pretty, black cheerleader who had been going steady with Matkins since he had arrived at Williams from Sellers. Evans' complaint was that the girl had been trying "to act white, and she's trying to get Matkins to do the same thing." One day Evans caught the pair cuddled in each other's arms (a popular stance among white Williams couples) in the hallway at a time when Matkins was supposed to be at practice. When Evans told the halfback to go to his office, the girl said, "He's with me now." Evans was furious. "Well, he may be with you permanent," he declared, and left. Matkins' other difficulty was that he had always looked up to Evans in a fatherly way, and at Williams the coach was not able to devote as much attention to his star player. He was often aloof with the boy, which confused him. "I couldn't spend as much time with him as I did at Sellers," said Evans, "because the whites would think I was playing favorites. But I don't know whether Larry understood this or not."

The problem with Freddy Long was more touchy. Long was a stocky youngster with a perpetually dazed, open-mouthed expression. Thanks to Frye's constant badgering, Long had produced startling offensive performances during the previous year. But he did this by calling hardly a play at the line of scrimmage himself; he was simply acting as his coach's alter ego. During the 1970 season Jerome Evans failed to get the same performances from Freddy Long. In fact, without Frye's hassling, Long seemed unable to function in the most elementary manner. When Evans gave him the freedom to call most of the plays, Long became confused. He would drop back for a pass, see a man clear, and then hesitate for fear his pass might be intercepted. Then, with opposing linemen bearing down on him, he would begin scrambling in all directions before finally being tackled for a huge loss. When he got up from the tackle, always with an agonizing slowness, he would glance over at Evans, as if awaiting instruction. Evans did not want to have to call plays. He wanted his quarterbacks to be independent. But only when he began to call the team's plays did Long's performance improve.

Evans could not bench the quarterback, since Long retained a reputation as a star from the previous year. The alternative was to have a serious talk with the boy. Evans shunned this course of action for a number of games. He did not want to impose himself on the boy, for one thing, and for another, he did not particularly like Freddy Long. After one game in which Long had kicked three field goals, the boy had shaken hands with each assistant coach until he reached Evans' out-stretched hand, which he avoided. Evans said nothing. Nor did Evans complain that although most quarter-backs stand beside their coach on the sidelines, it was Long's habit to sit as far away from Evans as possible. If Evans wanted him he would have to call for him two or three times before Long would move toward him.

Evans finally decided on a confrontation. He exhorted the quarterback to take more charge of the situation on the field. Long nodded. Evans suggested he speak up in the pregame pep talks and team meetings. Long nodded again. Evans said a few more things and then allowed him to leave. The coach felt relieved to be rid of the boy but dissatisfied. It was partly his own fault, Evans thought. But he wondered just how he was supposed to deal with people he felt truly hated him.

By his very nature, Evans muted antagonisms and muffled anxieties, so that the team as a whole had no complaints against him. And because both blacks and whites accepted their coach, they learned to accept one another. But this acceptance, although amicable, was precarious at best. It boiled down to a grudging realization by both blacks and whites that if they wanted the team to be successful they had to accommodate themselves to one another's individuality. This was nothing new for blacks, who long before had learned to accommodate themselves to the white world. But it was a new and startling realization for whites. For the first time, they had to acknowledge the existence of blacks, with that existence being as equal and as deserved as their own. Whites called no one "boy" and made blacks the butt of few jokes. They made a point of avoiding criticism; when a black player dropped an easy pass nothing would be said.

This stiff sense of acceptance was mirrored in the relationships of the team's integrated cheerleading squad. (By now there were nine whites and five blacks on the squad.) The cheerleaders took their cue from the football players, many of whom were boyfriends. The girls formed friendly if not affectionate relationships in a way only girls can—smiling, breathless, squealing, polite—with members of their own sex they do not particularly like or trust.

Any difficulties the two races encountered seemed more rooted in life-styles than in race. The black girls

seemed bewildered by the importance the whites attached to cheerleading. For the blacks, cheerleading was
a small part of their lives, an end in itself, something to
be enjoyed for the moment because it would lead to
nothing else. They did not see the social relations of
things, one to another, because for so long blacks had
been denied the results of their acts or abilities. For
example, being an intelligent black in Burlington in no
way guaranteed a man a job commensurate with his
abilities, as it did a white. So, for the same reason, the
black cheerleaders viewed cheerleading solely as a
casual endeavor, not a step forward—or upward.

The whites, on the other hand, were extremely conscious of the ties between things. Cheerleading, just like
athletic talent, beauty, and intelligence, could be extremely valuable to them in later years. It might lead to a
successful marriage, a career, and so on. For this reason
the whites treated cheerleading with a reverence that
seemed disproportionate to the blacks. The whites had
thought the 1969 riot had been started because of the
blacks' desire to become cheerleaders. If so, why were
the black girls now cutting practice and not fulfilling
their squad responsibilities? The answer lay not in the
blacks' desire to be cheerleaders, but in their wish to
have a part of anything they felt whites attached importance to, as if that thing had some mysterious and hidden value that would be revealed to them once they
possessed it. They accepted its importance completely
on the testimony of whites. But once they possessed it,

the black girls began to wonder what was so special about this thing they now had.

The superficial acceptance black and white football players, coaches and cheerleaders shared for one another also affected the relationships of the Williams students, teachers and parents and citizens of Burlington. They accepted one another because they all accepted Jerome Evans, who had consciously presented a low profile that had made him palatable to the most hardened segregationists. Whatever else even the hardcore segregationists felt toward him, they were forced to admit he was, to use their toughest phrase, "a decent nigger." Evans achieved this by refusing to force himself on anyone. He avoided trouble. If he saw parents or teachers who wanted nothing to do with him, he did not burden them with unnecessary smiles or pleasantries. But neither was he critical of them.

The impression Jerome Evans leaves in his wake is narcotic, tranquilizing but temporary. It has no substance. Once its effect wears off, people discover they are left with nothing tangible of Jerome Evans to add to their knowledge or experience, no word or deed or thought they can grasp and make their own, and thus allow themselves to transfer to Evans their allegiance. Evans' personality is devoted not to allegiances but to safety. In the back of his mind he deals always with the thought of potential enemies, never with the thought of potential friends. His policy is defensive, to leave people with nothing they can use against him.

Henry Crawford, the president of the Williams Booster Club and a man who had a prominent role in the effort to reinstate Frye just months before, declared in midseason he had no complaints against Evans. "I got along very well with Frye," said Crawford, a gray-haired businessman. "He had a clique of rooters, and I guess I was one of them. Jerome, he doesn't have any clique. He's more aloof with everyone. A lot of people like him for this, and I personally can't complain. So far he's handled himself wonderfully. The parents like him."

Not all the Boosters were as effusive in their praise. Lou Jones had been a friend of Frye's since 1956. For twenty years he carried the sideline chains at all home games. In 1970 he relinquished that duty to a Williams student.

"I guess Evans was the best-qualified one of the bunch if you want to look at it that way," said Jones. "Some don't like it any, but they ain't saying nothing. One father told me, 'My boys'll never play for no nigger, Lou.' Then one day in the paper Evans was quoted as saying the man's two sons would be real helpful to the club this year. Both sons are playing for Evans. When I asked the man why, he looked sheepish and said, 'Hell, Lou, that nigger's got a lot on the ball, you know.'

"Things ain't the same this year. Last season at the weekly Booster Club meetings Frye would introduce the Bulldog Player of the Week and then send the boy home and we'd all loosen up with a few jokes. Evans lets the boys hang around all night, and it makes us uncom-

fortable. And it seems Evans can't wait to get out of the
meetings himself. If Marilyn Monroe was stripping
naked on television you couldn't get Frye out of Booster
Club meetings. But even when Evans is there he doesn't
ever seem to loosen up. I'd like him a lot better if he
did."

By late October the Williams team was assured of a
winning record. The Bulldogs were 6–2 with two games
left, and about the only question remaining was would
they win their conference title and then go on to the
state tournament? Although most white players acted as
if a conference title and a state championship were their
sole reasons for being, much of their enthusiasm
seemed an effort. As one player put it then, "I'm tired of
football. If Dudley wins the title, I'll cry like everybody
else just to put on a good show, but I'll be glad as hell.
The only reason I played this year was because Evans
didn't make us cut our hair as Frye would have. Right
now, I'm sick of football."

Although most white players would not express
themselves this candidly, they seemed to share the
viewpoint. They were tired of living each day consciously, with no recourse to instinct and habit that had
marked their days before Evans' arrival. They were tired
of being aware of their every word and act, tired of
liking blacks, of liking their coach, tired in fact of all the
pressures that had been theirs since the year's first practice session. They seemed anxious to simplify what had
been a complex year in their lives, to plant their feet

once again on solid ground with horizons that were familiar and obstacles that were cleanly defined.

That was why, after their seventh victory of the season and only a week before the final game, a number of white players got together one night and drank Ripple wine and vodka into the following morning. By noon they were drunk. Someone suggested they drive to Gibsonville to see Frye. When they arrived, according to some of the boys who talked about the visit later, they waited nervously in his tiny office, not sure just how Frye would take their call. He appeared, smiling. There were handshakes and backslapping, and it was obvious he was glad to see his former players. He was pleased they still thought enough of him to make the trip to Gibsonville and to know he still had a firm bond with these boys, one which Evans had not broken.

A player complained offhandedly about something Evans had done in practice. Frye called him "a dumb nigger" and added that the Bulldogs should never have lost to all-black Dudley High, which they had done three Fridays before. The players agreed. There was a momentary silence in which each boy seemed to be wrestling with something that made him feel uneasy about what was happening. One of them said Frye was right, Evans was a dumb nigger. Someone else asked, "What could you expect from them? They are inferior." Other players chimed in, and there was an almost audible sigh of relief around the room as the boys relaxed and began to talk easily with their former coach. A player told Frye that the previous day there nearly had been a riot at Williams.

"What the hell you boys doing here, then?" said Frye. "I expect my boys to be in the thick of any trouble."

The players assured him they would be in the thick of such a fight. And when Frye asked if any of those niggers had made a move toward his daughter (a Williams senior) they told him that he didn't have to worry about that. They would make sure she was safe. Frye smiled and nodded.

"You know, we probably would have gone on to the state championship if you were still our coach," said one boy.

"We would not have lost a game," maintained a second.

Shortly before 1 P.M. the players said they had to leave. They were no longer drunk and were beginning to feel the unpleasant effects of a hangover.

"Ya all come back," said Frye as they piled into their cars. They said they would. "And watch out for my Cathy," Frye added, cementing the bond. "I need you guys."

"Don't you worry, coach," said a player, and they drove off. They felt satisfied at first and then less so, and by the time they reached Burlington they had begun to feel guilty, as if they had been a party to some unmanly act, had perpetrated some deceit, not only against Jerome Evans, whom they had befriended during the year, but also against C. A. Frye, in whom they had helped sustain an illusion of something that no longer existed. They were bewildered. Their visit to Frye had not simplified things after all. Far from it. They had returned to familiar ground only to find that ground no longer familiar, and now they were not sure where to turn.

The next Friday Williams won its final game, ending its season with an 8–2 record—the school's best performance in ten years. Shortly after that last game Mike Pierce talked about Coach Evans: "You don't have much to say to him outside of football. I feel sorry for him now that the season is over. Who'll talk to him? I never know what to say to him. I can't get into him. Whenever I get close he gives me that little smile of his, like a spider's web tightening. The best he's got from whites in Burlington is a kind of acceptance and indifference. If he got fired tomorrow, people'd say, 'That's too bad. The nigger was a pretty good coach, wasn't he? I wonder who'll get his job. Maybe we'll get Frye back.'"

Dr. Proffitt substantially agreed. "I doubt if whites will ever feel emotionally committed to Jerome Evans as they were to Frye," he said. "But that's his strength. I wanted a pragmatist at Williams, not a flag-waver. Evans would need to be a wonderfully sophisticated organism to perform the type of job he's done and still attract people emotionally. His job wasn't to deal with people on a personal level but as a representative of the blacks.

What annoyed me was that everyone talked all year about how much more appealing Frye was than Evans. But damn it, style isn't as important as substance. A person's charisma is frequently irrelevant to his ability to get a job done. So Frye was charismatic. Did people think this would get us safely through the year in this town? Shoot, I removed Frye not because he cussed a little but because I was afraid he would use his ability to get people emotionally committed to him in a cold and ruthless way—just as he tried to get his players to leave school for him without any thought to the boys' futures."

Epilogue

Jerome Evans and I are driving along Highway 85 toward Durham. It is a stiflingly hot Saturday, but in his new station wagon, with its humming air conditioner, it is chilly. Evans reaches over and pushes a button on the car radio. A man's voice is saying: "If you're 6 foot 8 and black, you don't have to play basketball in order to go to college anymore. You can obtain a student loan from North Carolina Mutual. . . ." Evans looks at me with a sly grin. "This is a black car," he says. "You ever ride in a black car before?"

"No, what makes it black?"

"All the radio buttons are set to black stations. That's all I listen to," and he punches another button. An announcer is giving the starting lineups for the North

Carolina Central vs. Charlotte-Smith football game. Both are black schools. "We're late," says Evans, and he presses down on the accelerator.

This is the first time Jerome Evans and I have gone out socially. Although we have gotten along as well as, if not better than, we expected in the weeks I have been in town, he has repeatedly declined suggestions that he and his family go out to dinner with me. "It isn't necessary," he would say. When I had first come to Burlington, with Evans' approval, to write a book, he avoided me constantly. He was often an hour late for scheduled interviews, and sometimes failed to show up entirely. Finally, in exasperation, I asked him why he consented to have the book written when obviously he had no stomach for the project. "It's my insurance policy," he said, and then went on to explain that if it were written down, plain to see, that he had not made one single mistake, one error of judgment, it would be impossible for him to be fired.

As we approached Durham we passed cars filled with well-dressed whites waving University of North Carolina banners. "My assistant coaches wanted me to go to the UNC game," Evans says. "I told them I'd promised to take you to see NCC to play. You were a good excuse to get out of their invitations."

"Thanks a lot."

"What's there for me, anyway?" he says. "Nothing. They'll all be white, and I won't be able to relax. And when they go to those postgame parties, what am I gonna do, start talking to some white girl? Wouldn't that be beautiful? Everyone in Burlington would be saying Jerome Evans wants a white girl. They'd love that. No sir, I'd rather go to NCC. I know everyone there. I feel comfortable. I'm no black separatist or anything like that. But it's too late for me, I'll never mix. I've got a lot of hate buried in me and I want to keep it buried. If I mix too much it might come out.

"I'm satisfied with the way things are. More than satisfied. I've reached my goal in life. I don't want to go any higher. I'll let other blacks become leaders of my people. I'd lived in the black world for so long, I had no desire to leave it. Then they closed Sellers, and I had to. Everything that happened this year was new to me. But now that I'm dealing with whites, I don't care if they like me or not. I don't even want them to like me. I'd be content if they just acknowledged me as a good coach and a man."

The NCC campus consists of modern brick buildings spread over rolling hills. In a valley sits the football stadium. It really is not a stadium but wooden stands on either side of a field that has a number of brown patches on it. The buildings, the field, and the campus remind me of the few black homes I have visited in Burlington. They are new, plain and functional, without any signs of a tradition or culture of their own.

We walk through the gate, admitted on Evans' coach's pass, and someone calls out "Little Willie, how's my man?" Evans smiles at a heavyset black and then says to me, "My nickname in college. Would you believe he was a teammate of mine? He's gotten fat."

Evans excuses himself for a minute and goes to the men's room. I am standing in an open space between the field and the entrance gate. To the right is a tent where black women are barbecuing spareribs. The smell of sweet sauce and burning pork is all about me. The game is in progress, the two teams huddled over the ball near the 50-yard line. They are all black. The referees, tall, raw-boned men in spotless white pants and black-and-white-striped shirts, are black. Patrolling the sidelines, just as at every football game in the country, are over-age, paunchy policemen. They too are black. Behind what must have been the NCC goal a group of black women are watching a mass of children playing in the leaves. On a rise overlooking the field a group of black men are standing, talking, arguing and laughing, and passing paper cups of rum back and forth. The stands are filled with 10,000 people: older men—alumni—in suits with hair that is slicked and gleaming; their women, plump, pants-suited, with straight hair upturned at the ends; younger men—students—with Afros, goatees, berets, sunglasses, and sullen faces; young women in dungaree bell-bottoms and tight sweaters, with bushy Afros and that pouty Angela Davis look that has become popular.

Suddenly I am aware that my face is the only white one among these thousands of blacks. Evans has not returned. There is a fluttery feeling in my stomach, the

kind actors must get before they go onstage before a
vast audience. My head feels light, airy, as it must be
with pot, and for the first time in my life I am acutely
conscious of myself, of my presence, of existing somehow differently from those around me. I feel everyone
must notice this difference, and that is why they stare. A
girl walks by on the arm of her boyfriend. They do not
even cast a curious glance in my direction. Was that
deliberate? Three more girls pass, one looking quickly
over her shoulder and then whispering to her friends,
who begin to giggle among themselves.

When Evans reappears I relax slightly, but as we walk
toward the stands I feel a tightening in my facial muscles
and realize that for some insane reason I am smiling at
his every word. When we reach the edge of the stands I
am momentarily terrified. Is he going to lead me past all
those black faces until he finds a seat on the 50-yard
line? I can see them turning, an entire bleacher of black
faces riveted to me as I walk past. But, mercifully, Evans
sees a seat just above and begins climbing between
people, motioning for me to follow. I step onto the first
plank; a black man slides away without looking up at me.
Was he angry that my foot almost touched his coat,
annoyed, indifferent? I move between people who
make room for my feet until halfway up, there is no
opening. I am standing idiotically in front of a girl who
does, really does, resemble Angela Davis. She makes
believe she does not notice me. "Excuse me," I say.
Again that uncontrollable smile. "Excuse me," I say

louder, maybe too loud, I think. She looks up, unsmil-
ing, and moves over. "Thank you," I say, and step
quickly to the top of the bleachers where Evans has
made a place for me a little apart from the other fans. I
sit down, sweating, mentally exhausted from that climb.

I do not recall much of the game. It is a blur. I remember only being so conscious of my presence among
those black faces that I did not say one word or raise a
hand to scratch an itch or cross a leg without first replay-
ing the word or act over and over in my mind until I was
sure that it was an acceptable word or act and that certainly no one about me could take exception to it. I do
remember Evans talking a lot and getting so engrossed
in the game that he began yelling, "You stupid, boy, you
just plain stupid" every time one of the NCC players
fumbled or dropped a pass. I remember also the NCC
band coming on the field at halftime, twisting and sing-
ing, and Evans telling me that once the school's
bandleader had tried to get the group to perform like a
white band and they were booed loudly by the fans.
When the majorettes appeared in shimmering tights,
the crowd began cheering and clapping. The girls began
to twist, and a man a few seats down from us looked
through his binoculars and started hollering, "Lorda
mercy, Lorda mercy, I was born twenty years too soon."

"Hey, man, let me at those things," said Evans. The
man handed him the glasses. Evans looked down at the
girls and said to no one in particular, "Now, that's one
helluva game. Yes sir, one helluva game down there."

The man who owned the glasses laughed.

We left before the game was over. I followed Evans down the bleachers, making sure to move directly into the cleared spaces people made for him. He led me past the middle-aged men who had stood throughout the game on the rise at one end of the field. They waved and called to him.

"I usually stand over there at the games," Evans told me, "although lately they've been kidding me because I won't drink much with them. They say that since I got the job at Williams I've gone white. I try to remind them that I never drank that much at our games. But they'll never believe me now that I have showed up with a white man. You know, you gonna get me in trouble. Ruin my name in the community," and he started laughing.

Was he kidding, I wondered. Or was he really ashamed to stand with his friends because of me?

When we arrived back in Burlington it was still light. I got out of the car, thanking Evans for taking me along. He said it was nothing and drove off. Across the street I could see William, the colored boy who served as the bellhop for the Alamance Motel. William, who is over seventy, was helping a white man take the luggage out of his car. As I crossed the street, I realized that I had relaxed considerably. I was on familiar ground again.

October 1971

An Angel of His Time

"My career?" he says with a shrug. "It was no big thing. I could never get the knack of what they wanted of me." He takes a delicate sip from a tall glass, purses his lips slightly, then continues. "Oh, I might have had a career if they could have tied me to the mast. You know, like Ulysses? When he heard the mermaids' wailing he wanted to crash against the rocks." He raises his glass to his ear and shakes it gently until the ice cubes tinkle. "You know, Babe—like vodka on the rocks." He smiles. His eyebrows are raised and his mouth is pulled back and down into his jaw. It is a self-mocking smile. It distrusts itself. It is the smile of a man who is accustomed to looking at himself from outside of himself, who takes what he sees with such slight regard that he can smile not at his pun, which is almost cruelly close to the mark, but at the man who can make such a pun.

51

There is a photograph of Robert "Bo" Belinsky in the May 6, 1962, edition of *The Sporting News*. A slick-looking young man in a California Angels' baseball uniform is surrounded by a number of aging baseball dignitaries and Angels' executives. The older men are dressed in business suits. They are smiling stiffly at the camera while Belinsky, his head cocked slightly to the left, one eyebrow raised, is smiling that slightly ironic, distrustful smile of his at the baseball he is holding up for view. With that baseball he has just recorded his fourth straight major league victory and history's first no-hit, no-run game by a rookie left-handed pitcher. That no-hitter will make Belinsky, at the age of twenty-five, the most celebrated athletic personality in the country. He will be courted by such Hollywood beauties as Ann-Margret and Mamie Van Doren, and he will eventually marry a *Playboy* Playmate of the Year. He will become an intimate of Hugh Hefner, Walter Winchell, Frank Sinatra, and J. Edgar Hoover. He will say to the press, "J. Edgar! Man, he's a swinger! He let me shoot tommy guns at FBI headquarters. I told him if I ever quit this game I might need a job. He said, 'Bo, there'll always be a place for you on the force.'"

Belinsky will also become the star in a prospective television series about a motorcycle loner named Buddy Solo, and in a Las Vegas nightclub act with Mamie Van Doren. Of her "Bo," Mamie will say, "I've got better curves than Bo, but he's got a heckuva better voice. I know, because he sings to me in his car."

Belinsky will be dogged and quoted voluminously by sportswriters, who recognized in him a unique and colorful personality who could always be counted on for such outrageous quips as: "If I'd known I was gonna pitch a no-hitter today I would have gotten a haircut"; or, "My only regret in life is that I can't sit in the stands and watch me pitch"; or, "My philosophy of life? That's easy: If music be the food of love, by all means let the band play on."

In short, within days after his no-hitter Robert "Bo" Belinsky, a former pool hustler from Trenton, N.J., would be heralded as sport's most original and engaging playboy–athlete. His name would become synonymous with a life-style that was cool and slick and dazzling, epitomizing not only the life-styles of such later athletes as Joe Namath, Ken Harrelson, and Derek Sanderson, but also those of an entire, ephemeral decade—the 1960s. And eventually, only a few short years later, that same name would become synonymous with dissipated talent.

Bo Belinsky won only 24 major league baseball games in the nine years following that rookie no-hitter. He lost 51 times. He was traded away by five major league clubs and fined, suspended, and banished to the minors regularly for what had come to be viewed as his unstable and childish behavior. Those same sportswriters who had written adoringly of the rakish Belinsky as a winner became less than adoring with Belinsky the loser.

"There is a race to Bo Belinsky's pad every morning," wrote one sportswriter. "It is a race to see who arrives there first, Belinsky or his milkman. Belinsky has yet to win." Another wrote, "The Angels are about to market a new Bo Belinsky doll. You wind it up and it plays all night, all morning, and three innings in the afternoon."

One morning Bo Belinsky was picked up by the police at five o'clock for throwing a female companion out of his moving "lipstick-red" Cadillac on Sunset Strip. The Angels fined him, and the girl sued him. On another morning at three o'clock Belinsky was accused of punching a sportswriter in his hotel room. For that incident he was suspended from the Angels and, without a hearing by the commissioner of baseball, immediately banished to the minor leagues. On still another morning, this time at four o'clock, the hotel in which Belinsky and his teammates were staying burned down. While his teammates assembled sleepily in the streets, the manager began to count heads. "My god!" screamed the manager. "He's not here! He must be inside." From behind the crowd a voice mumbled, "Who's inside?" The players and their manager turned around to confront Robert "Bo" Belinsky stepping from a cab, as he put it, "reeking of bitch and booze." The following morning Belinsky explained his fine to the press thusly: "Boys, you know you're going good when you beat a bed check and then your hotel burns down." His record at the time was 1 and 5.

One night Belinsky took a few friends to dinner at an

exclusive French restaurant. He ordered a bottle of wine. The waiter informed him that he was mispronouncing the name of the wine. "It is Châteauneuf-du-Pape," said the waiter. Belinsky looked up from his drink, his eyebrows raised inquisitively. "Oh, it is, is it?" And then he picked up the table, which was loaded with shrimp cocktails and bread sticks, and threw it through a window.

Eventually, events so turned on Belinsky that even Mamie Van Doren became disillusioned with her "Bo." One day she announced tearfully to a host of reporters that Bo and she were terminating their engagement. "I'm returning his ring," she said. "I'm afraid if I don't he'll cut off my finger and take it—or worse, make me take over the payments." Belinsky's response was characteristic. "Mamie's a good broad," he said to the press. "I still think she's got a little class—very little."

Despite growing public disenchantment with his behavior, Belinsky was undaunted. He denied that his acts were those of an unstable man. "I feel I'm very stable," he told a sportswriter. "Proof of which is that I'm still single. Only unstable guys get married." Shortly after that remark, Belinsky married Jo Collins, a *Playboy* playmate. That marriage ended prematurely one night when Belinsky tore a $500 wig from his wife's head and threw it onto Sunset Strip. "It just goes to show," he said afterwards, "you can't play hearts and flowers with a product of nudity."

Finally, on his thirtieth birthday, four years before he

would retire unnoticed from baseball, Bo Belinsky admitted publicly that his once-promising career had ceased to exist. (At the time he was struggling with a 1–5 record for the Houston Astros.) His career had collapsed, he said, under the weight of too many fines, suspensions, trades, and banishments to the minors—not to mention the weight of his own personality. And it seemed, he added, that each setback was inflicted on him just as he was about to reach his peak, until now, at thirty, there were no more peaks in sight. He also admitted that his public, which had found him an entertaining enough young man as a winner, had grown increasingly weary of, and finally annoyed with, what it felt was unstable and self-destructive behavior. As an aging and unsuccessful playboy, Bo Belinsky had become a parody of himself.

When a Houston sportswriter asked him how sport's most notorious playboy felt on reaching thirty, Bo replied with a smile. "Babe, it's no fun knowing that in every home in America your birthday is celebrated as a day of infamy." An exaggeration, perhaps, for it is doubtful whether anyone in America, including Belinsky himself, celebrated his birthday at all. However, that remark was telling. It was characteristically clever—one might say almost too clever. It seemed to have been delivered more for effect than truth by a man more concerned with style than substance. It was tossed off, discarded really, with an ironic smile of disavowal, as if to say it was nothing but the surplus from a warehouse of such remarks, remarks its author must unload whenever he felt the occasion deserved. Despite all this, one still had the annoying suspicion that Bo Belinsky felt his remark contained more truth than wit. It was not clear whether this feeling was the overblown self-pity of a too-shallow man or the heightened perception of a too-sensitive man. It was only clear that Robert "Bo" Belinsky had dissipated a promising career, that his public had grown weary of him, and that much of his difficulty could be traced to his personality. He did not have the knack of such later athletes of consciously cultivating his personality precisely up to, but not beyond, that point at which the public becomes bored with it.

Bo Belinsky, thirty-five years old, leans forward in his armchair to better examine the picture of himself holding that no-hit baseball of nine years past. With his fingertips he displaces a lock of hair from his forehead. It is an exquisite, almost delicate gesture done in slow motion. His hair is black. He wears it long and shaggy rather than slicked back and gleaming as he did nine years ago. Its blackness, coupled with his tanned skin and slightly flattened features, gives him the appearance of a man of Mexican descent. He is still darkly handsome, although his skin is no longer tight and sleek. There are small lines at the corners of his eyes and mouth. He is wearing only a cream-colored bathing suit with the word "Bo" scripted above the left leg.

He looks to be about 6'1" and 190 pounds—a gain of

10 pounds over the years. And yet, despite the added flesh spilling over the waist of his trunks, despite the tiny stubble of beard and the lines and the look of aging, somehow Bo Belinsky looks better than he did nine years ago. He looks truer, more substantial, as if the lines and added weight had forced on him dimensions and substance he did not have nine years ago, and which he had not consciously cultivated since. He looks less slick, less glossy, less conscious of his external self. He no longer possesses that pampered, self-satisfied look that gave one the impression that if you tried to grab hold of him your hands would slip off with the grease.

After his no-hitter his mother told reporters that her son worked out every day in a gym. "Bo just loves his body," she said. Today, a hot summer morning six months after his retirement from baseball, Bo Belinsky no longer "works out." As is his custom, he will do nothing more strenuous than sit for hours in the living room of this spacious ranch house tucked high into the Hollywood Hills overlooking Los Angeles. Possibly he will work out his horoscope. He is a Sagittarius. ("The most flexible sign in the universe," he says. "A Sag gets along with everyone.") But it makes little difference what his day's horoscope suggests (a long hike in the mountains?), for his routine will not vary. He will sit until noon in the shadow of the chimney centered in the living room so as to best avoid the sunlight pouring through the sliding glass doors to his left. He will sip steadily from the glass on the coffee table beside his armchair and, to amuse himself, will watch a morning quiz show; or answer the constantly ringing telephone; or just gaze at the many paintings, poems, camp artifacts, and photographs that litter the walls. Most of the photographs are of his friends, some in cowboy suits with drawn guns and pixy smiles, others bearded, with wind-blown hair and glazed, meditative looks. Throughout the day Belinsky will pass the time in an endless stream of gossip and small talk with those same friends who will drift into and out of this room over which he presides, the orchestrator of the day's unfolding.

It is nine o'clock in the morning and the room is occupied by about seven or eight people in various states of sprawl. All are strangely quiet, self-contained, as if this huge room was a universe and each person in it a planet unto himself, spinning in an orbit entirely his own. Most of them, including Belinsky, have yet to get to sleep after last night's party, which concluded only minutes ago.

To Belinsky's left on the other side of the coffee table sits a pudgy, gray-haired little man in his fifties. He is wearing striped bellbottoms and no shirt. His name is Phil. He works for a company that makes locks and burglar alarms. ("I've been trying to get him to give me the combinations," says Belinsky. "What a score, eh?") Phil is bent forward, his elbows on his knees, his face buried in his hands. He is moaning softly. Beside his chair, folded like a jacknife on the couch, sits a tall, slender girl in a flowered bikini. Bonnie is about eighteen, maybe seventeen. She has the face of a young Sophia Loren. Her chin is resting on her raised knee so she can best paint her toenails with complete self-absorption. Occasionally she will look up, wide-eyed, and blow a kiss in Belinsky's direction. He will smile back. ("A stray," he says, "I found her last night on the Strip. She says she wants to stay." He shrugs.)

Another girl in a flowered bikini is moving languidly about the room, collecting glasses, emptying ashtrays, dusting. She is older than Bonnie, maybe thirty, but also tall and cool. She is not quite so pretty. Linda has pale blue eyes, bright red hair, and a fleshy, but attractive, body. She too seems self-absorbed as she works, only her self-absorption seems less single-minded than does Bonnie's. ("Linda's a good chickie," says Bo. "She's got her share of patches.")

To the left of the couch, standing in front of the mirror above the leather-padded bar, is a small, lean man in his late thirties. He has fine, straight features, unblinking eyes, a long ponytail, and gray muttonchop sideburns. He is studiously fluffing out his sideburns with one hand, while with the other he adjusts the cartridge belt slung over one shoulder. His name is Chris. He is a prophet. Every afternoon at lunchtime he walks down to Schwab's drugstore on Sunset Strip, climbs onto a soap box, and, with his German shepherd panting beside him, preaches to the passersby. Today he will warn them that if they continue to worship material things they will never be able to see spiritual things. "Dead things are for blind people," he will say. And, "The jackals of hell will lick your blood from the streets." Then he will walk back to the house, prepare an organic lunch for himself and his dog, and watch "The Dating Game" on television. Sometimes he watches the news. But when he does he invariably ends up arguing with one of the commentators. It is not an uncommon sight to walk into the living room and see Chris standing with his finger poked at an image of David Brinkley, who is laconically reading from a paper as Chris shouts at him, "Distorter of facts! Harbinger of doom! Tool of corrupt establishments!" (Bo says of Chris, "He's all right. A little freaky, maybe, but aren't we all? He's got his little act, so what? Everybody's got a little act.")

To Chris's right, alongside the glass sliding doors that overlook a tear-shaped swimming pool one story below, a skinny little man in a white bathing suit is sleeping on a wall couch. Awake, he is skittish, quick-witted, caustic. His name is Len and he owns this house in which Belinsky is staying. ("Len's a gas," says Belinsky. "He's the unofficial mayor of Los Angeles.") Len's presence on the couch is making it difficult for the painter to reach the wall behind him. The painter has been painting that same wall for six days. Every so often he pauses and glances out the glass doors at the swimming pool below. Two girls are sunning themselves beside the pool. They are both lying on their backs, each with the back of a hand flattened across her eyes. Both girls are wearing only the bottoms of their bikinis. ("He went freaky the first time he looked out that window," says Belinsky of the painter. "He's been painting that same wall ever since. I think we'll send *him* a bill!")

At about noon Belinsky and his friends, some of whom are sleeping in other rooms throughout the house, will join those two girls beside the pool. Belinsky will sit by the pool "taking some color" until one of his friends sneaks up behind him and pushes him into the pool, or until he feels sweat seeping from his body, in which case he will dive in to cool himself, emerging quickly and returning to his deck chair. But noon is still hours away.

Belinsky puts down the picture of himself and sits back in his chair. "What was I thinking then?" he says. "I was thinking, 'Man, a no-hitter, that's nice! I wonder what happens next?' I mean, a no-hitter, it's nice but it's no big thing." He picks up his glass, takes a sip and returns it to the table. "Sure, I would have liked to have had a career after that. But I never thought I would. I knew there's always someone waiting around the corner to take a shot at you. It's just a matter of time. Besides, there's no way I could have done anything different—I mean, lived my life differently. Can a leopard change his spots? You can shave all the fur off the poor bastard and he's still got his spots, right? Who can explain it? Why does a mad dog howl at the moon? Why did I do the things I did?" He smiles, picks up his glass and drains it.

He motions with it toward the tall redhead who has been tidying up. "Heh, Babe, some more Wheaties?"

Linda looks up from her dusting. "Sure, Bo." She moves to his chair and bends over to take his glass. Her breasts strain against the top of her bikini. Bo looks up, shakes his head once. "All right, Babe! That's all right!" Linda, poised over him, looks down at her breasts and then to Belinsky. They both smile, that identical, knowing, self-mocking smile. Linda takes his glass and straightens up. She tosses her long red hair from her eyes and laughs a noiseless laugh that comes in spurts, like breaths. "Bo, you're too much," she says. She turns her back on him and moves off in a languid, loose-hipped shuffle. Belinsky follows her with his eyes, shaking his head and saying, "So many broads, man, so many broads. It's a shame . . . heh, what's that poem, 'Give me ten stouthearted men, and soon I'll have ten thousand more.' Well, make mine chickies. Yes sir, make mine chickies," and he laughs. He slides down into his chair, only the top of his head visible, and he laughs.

When his laughter fades he is silent for a while, smiling to himself. Absentmindedly he begins curling a lock of hair at the back of his head. Finally he says, "My problem was simple, Babe. I heard music nobody else heard." As he speaks he is staring straight ahead at the chimney. "I remember once I was playing in the Texas League when the team bus stopped in Veracruz so we could eat. All the players went into the restaurant except me. I thought I heard music down the street so I

went looking for it. I found a two-piece jazz band playing on the sidewalk in front of a bar. I listened for a
while, and when they went inside I followed them. I had
a few drinks and then I left. I had every intention of
returning to that bus until I ran into another jazz band
down the street. I followed them into a bar too. What I
didn't know was that all these bars hired jazz bands to
lure customers inside. Man, after that bar, it seemed like
every step I took there were these damned buglers waiting just for me. 'Here he comes!' they seemed to be
saying. 'Get ready, here he comes!' . . . I woke up six
days later in a hotel room in Acapulco. I had a sponsor.
This blonde Mexican broad—she had to be blonde,
right!—was sitting by the bed saying, 'Belinsky! Belinsky! I make you great Yanqui bullfighter! But first we
must change your name.' I said, 'Sure, Babe. We'll
change it to Lance. Lance Belinsky, how's
that?' . . . My team? They were in Mexico City. We
passed each other going in opposite directions. It was
always like that with me."

It is 10 o'clock now. The sun has begun to move from
behind the chimney into Belinsky's path. It streams in
through the glass doors and momentarily blinds him. He
raises one hand to shade his eyes. With the other he
searches across the coffee table for his sunglasses. When
he finds them he puts them on. "That's better," he says.
"Too much sun. Too much . . ." Then suddenly he
says, "I don't feel sorry for myself. No way. I knew
sooner or later I'd have to pay the piper. You can't beat

the piper, Babe. I never thought I could. But I'll tell you who I do feel sorry for." He leans over the arm of his chair, furtively looking left and right as if afraid the others will eavesdrop on this secret he is about to impart. A meaningless gesture. They are oblivious to him. Satisfied no one is listening, he turns and says softly, "I feel sorry for all those poor bastards who never heard music." He laughs out loud. "Those poor fucking bastards!" and he falls back into his chair laughing.

The doorbell rings. Linda, returning with Bo's drink, goes to the door. It is the telephone repairman. Linda leads him to the glass doors overlooking the pool. The painter sighs disgustedly, as if severely hampered in his work by this crush of people about him. He begins feverishly slapping the wall with his brush. Linda points down at the swimming pool. The telephone repairman looks down for a very long moment. Then he looks at Linda.

"How did they get in the swimming pool?" he says.

Linda shrugs. "There was a call for Lloyd Bridges," and she walks over to Belinsky and hands him his drink.

"A call for Lloyd Bridges?" Bo repeats. "That's trippy, Babe. That's real trippy." He takes his glass, raises it before his eyes and says with a smile, "To amnesia." He sips delicately, then puts the glass on the table. He picks up a book of famous quotations and begins flipping through the pages. He is looking for the source of the quotation, "Give me ten stouthearted men. . . ."

Meanwhile, the telephone man has found the sockets

out of which the two white telephones had been re-moved. He looks over his shoulder and says to no one in particular, "The phones were ripped out of the wall."

Belinsky looks over at him, his eyebrows raised, and says, "Is that a fact, Babe? Ripped out, huh?" He shakes his head in disbelief and goes back to his book. It was Belinsky who had removed the telephones from the wall only hours ago. When he had come home from an all-night party he had been met at the door by Phil, who told him he'd been kept awake all night long answering calls from such friends of Bo's as Hollywood Mike, Chicago Danny, and Red-Headed Mike.

"A new arrangement must be worked out with the telephones," said Phil.

Belinsky replied, "Sure, Babe," and walked over to the telephones, ripped them out of the wall and threw them through the sliding glass doors (which, fortu-nately, were opened) into the deepest part of the swim-ming pool.

It was not Belinsky's disagreement with Phil that pre-cipitated his outburst, however. Its seeds had been sown much earlier in the evening when Bo, Len, and three male friends had begun their nightly rounds of Sunset Strip nightclubs. They stopped first at a favorite haunt just as three of that club's exotic dancers, dressed only in their nightgowns, were being ushered into a police car. The girls' arrest stemmed from an act they had just performed on stage while three crew-cut members of the L.A. vice squad watched from a darkened corner table. The act centered around one girl who took a bath on stage and was soon joined in her tub by the other two who washed her back. "It's a helluva act," said Belinsky as the police car drove off.

Disappointed but undaunted, Belinsky and his party went on to The Sportspage, a hangout for professional athletes, and then on to The Candy Store, a Beverly Hills discotheque frequented by Hollywood celebrities. At both places Belinsky's party was virtually ignored. They were seated at darkened tables far removed from the action. Belinsky himself went essentially unrecognized except for two isolated incidents. At The Sportspage he was approached by a pot-bellied man who wanted him to play on his Sunday morning softball team. "A great way to stay in shape," said the man. "We have free beer after the game." At The Candy Store Belinsky was approached by a gray-haired man dressed entirely in white, like Tom Mix, who said he was a movie producer who wanted to make a film of Belinsky's life.

"I have just the title," said Belinsky. "We'll call it, 'A Funny Thing Happened on the Way to a Career.'"

The man in white said, "That's good, Bo. That's very, very good. Maybe you can play yourself. Can you act?"

"Have I got an act!" replied Belinsky.

At about midnight Belinsky and his friends got up to leave The Candy Store. Len pointed to a man leaning against the wall near the doorway. "Catch his act," said Len. "He's doing an imitation of Hugh Hefner." The man had chalky-white skin. He was wearing a purple velvet jumpsuit and smoking a pipe. His arms were folded across his chest as if he were hugging himself. His act turned out not be an act, however, and after a few words of greeting Hugh Hefner invited Belinsky and as many friends as he could muster to a party at his Beverly Hills mansion.

"I'm bored tonight," said Hefner as he led Belinsky and Len to his Rolls Royce. "Barbie's in the hospital and I could use some company."

By the time Hugh Hefner's black limousine reached the electronically controlled gate that opened to a winding driveway that led eventually to his $3.5 million Tudor castle, it was being trailed by nearly a dozen Fords, Chevys, and Pontiacs of various age and hue. The cars were filled with about thirty casual friends of Belinsky's, most of whom were small-time hustlers and gamblers operating along Sunset Strip.

The party at the Elizabethan castle began at 2 A.M., with Hefner leading his guests on a tour of his possessions. He showed them his gleaming kitchen where his cooks (like all his servants, on 24-hour call) were preparing a snack for them. He showed them his bed, his game room, his projection room, his vast, neatly clipped grounds discriminantly dotted with intimate little lovers' parks. And finally he showed them his as yet uncompleted swimming pool, which was the size of a small lake. Because the pool was nothing more than a huge dirt- and boulder-strewn ditch, Hefner led his guests

back inside where he produced an architect's drawing of
the finished product. The pool would eventually resemble one of those lush jungle hide-aways seen so often on
men's after-shave commercials on television. It would
be planted with overhanging tropical foliage and tanned,
bikini'd bunnies. (The bunnies were shown in various
poses—lying on a rock, sunning their already brown
bodies, one knee languorously raised.)

When Hefner had shown his guests all the possessions he felt they should see, he led them to the living
room, where his servants had spread out a snack of red
and black caviar, strawberries and melon, assorted
cheeses and bottles of champagne. By then his guests
had grown ravenous with hunger—only their hunger
was not for the food surrounding them but for the opu-
lent life-style they had just devoured with their eyes.
Their quick hustlers' minds clicked into gear. They
searched frantically for a way, as Belinsky put it, "To
hitch a ride on that big bunny bird in the sky." The men
began talking loudly about "deals" and "scores" they
could make if only they had the proper "backing." The
women, urged on by their boyfriends, passed behind
Hefner and stooped to whisper in his ear about "deals"
of their own, about "scores" they had in mind—such as
being able to stencil across their navals tomorrow morning, "Property of Hugh Hefner Enterprises."

"It was an orgy," said Belinsky afterwards. "Everyone
was climbing each others' back to buzz in Hefner's ear."

Throughout the frenzy, however, Hefner remained

impassive. He sat Indian-style on a velvet pillow on the floor, his guests spread out before him. His arms were folded across his chest; his pipe alternately dangled from one hand or was clenched between his teeth; his small black eyes darted from guest to guest, the eyes reading but unreadable. He did not say more than a dozen words all morning (as if somehow his daily allotment had been exhausted on his guided tour), but instead contented himself with watching the anguished strivings of those about him. Like some voyeur of human anxieties, he seemed to actually take pleasure in the sweaty brows and clenched stomachs of his guests. Throughout the morning his head bobbed forward mechanically, like a string puppet's, although it bobbed not in approval to the words of his guests (as they mistakenly believed) but in silent affirmation to some private truth he took great pleasure in seeing verified before his eyes.

From a distant corner of the room, seated alone, Belinsky watched the proceedings silently. As the morning wore on he grew sullen. Unsure of the source of his anger, he began to drink heavily. At dawn he saw Hefner stand up suddenly, thank his guests for coming and leave the room. The guests looked dazedly at each other. The, half-drunk, half-asleep, unsure of what next was expected of them, they rose unsteadily and began to wander out of the house into a chill and foggy morning.

When Belinsky and Len returned to Len's house in Hollywood Hills, Phil met Bo at the door and complained about the telephones. "What followed," said Len with a grin, "was a typical Polack rage."

Belinsky puts down the book of quotations and says, "Going to Hefner's house was no big thing for me. I've known the guy for years. He offered me a job, but I turned it down. I never went much for that Playboy philosophy and stuff. I'm not one for institutionalized sex. I mean, you don't use women, Babe, you compliment them. They compliment you. How can you use a woman? We all climbed out of a womb, right? But still, Heff's a gracious host. I wanted my friends to enjoy themselves last night. It was a score for them, something they could talk about for a week. Instead, they tried to hock his silverware. The stupid bastards!"

Bo sips from his glass, then sips again, and finally says with raised eyebrows, "I met my wife through Heff. She's one reason I quit baseball. I've got this thing going with her, a divorce action. It's no big thing but it started to get me down a little. I haven't done much these past months except try to get amnesia." He raises his glass and smiles. "But it was my own fault. Some guys love to get their dummy knocked by a broad. And to top it off, she's a Leo. Man, those Leo broads are very tough. Very self-righteous. Always reminding you of how *you* blew it. Ha! As if you needed reminding! I split finally when she said she wanted to be a bunny den mother at the Playboy Club in Denver. How's that, Babe, trippy? A bunny mother? What'd that make me, a bunny daddy?"

While Bo speaks, the room and its occupants remain essentially unchanged. It is now 11 A.M. Len is still sleeping by the glass doors while the painter and telephone repairman work around him. Linda is still tidying up in that floating, ethereal way of hers. Phil is still moaning into his hands. Bonnie is still painting her toenails. Chris, the prophet, is the only person to have altered his orbit. He is sitting cross-legged on the floor, leafing through pages of notes he will use for this afternoon's sermon at Schwab's drugstore. Satisfied, Chris reaches for the one available telephone Belinsky somehow missed in his earlier rage, and begins dialing. He asks the operator to put him through to Secretary of State Rogers. "In Washington, D.C.," he adds. Belinsky stops talking and motions toward Chris with his glass. He raises a finger to his lips and in an exaggerated manner cocks an ear. Chris tells the operator he is trying to locate the sacred Hopi burial grounds. "It's somewhere in the Mojave desert," he says. "The Secretary would know. What? This is Chris. Tell him Chris is calling."

Belinsky shakes his head and laughs silently to himself. He sips the last of his drink and then shakes the glass so the ice cubes tinkle. Linda looks over and nods. Bo does not begin talking again until Linda returns with another full glass.

"My wife wasn't the only reason I quit," he says. "You could say I no longer heard 'The Tunes of Glory.' I never liked baseball that much, at first anyway. I only signed a contract to get out of Trenton. Things were getting a little tacky for me there. I was hustling pool and hanging around with some bad people. At the time $185 a month and a ticket to some witches' monastery in Pancakesville, Ga., didn't look so bad. I quit baseball a number of times over the years, but for one reason or another I always came back. I almost quit in the spring of 1962. The Angels wanted me to sign a standard rookie contract and I refused. Then a few months later I pitched the no-hitter. The rest is history. I threatened to quit a few times after that no-hitter, like when they shipped me to Hawaii for hitting that sportswriter. It was like they were sending me into exile. I felt disconnected from things, so I threatened to quit. But that was just a bluff on my part.

"There was no way I could quit. I had learned to love the game by then. That's funny, isn't it, Babe? Me, the guy everybody said didn't love the game enough. Ha! I ended up devoting 15 years of my life to baseball. Man, I loved the fucking game. I just didn't take it seriously, that's all. I mean, Babe, I don't take myself seriously, how could I take a game seriously. It's just a game for little boys. To play it you've got to be a little boy at heart. The problem is some of these apples—you know, jocks—take it too seriously. They let the game define them. They become, say, a great hitter, and they begin to think of themselves as great in ways that have nothing to do with their baseball talent. They define themselves in ways they aren't. They get a little act and they take it all so fucking seriously.

"I never let any game define me. I was serious when I pitched, but once off that mound I defined myself. So what if I loved a few broads or took a drink? That didn't make me a bad guy, did it? I tried to live my life the way I wanted, with a little style, a little creativity. In the long run it wore me down, physically and mentally. Not the playing around, but fighting those bastards who misunderstood me. The apples said I was bad for the game. My managers were always trying to straighten me out. They'd call me into their office and try to read my act. You know, 'Come on, kid, what seems to be bothering you? You can tell me, I'm on your side.' And when I opened up, when I stood there with my insides hanging out, they buttoned themselves up. The next day they'd run to the front office and I'd get shipped to the minors again. Those bastards! They wouldn't pull dead rats off their own mothers!"

He takes a sip from his glass, calms himself, and then continues. "It was then I realized this wasn't a man's game. Men chase broads and get drunk and are straight with you. They don't have an act. They aren't hypocrites. For example, when I was going with Mamie they called me into the office every day and told me she was no good for me. Finally, when I wouldn't listen, they shipped my ass to Hawaii. And while I'm there I get this call from Mamie telling me that the same front office

people who shipped me out were trying to rip her off
while I'm gone." He smiles and nods his head. "Is that
trippy or isn't it? . . . If only I didn't see that shit I
would have been all right. But I had this goddamned
third eye, and when I saw things I shouldn't have I
overreacted. Usually it was in a way that made no sense,
like getting drunk or something. Maybe I'm too sensi-
tive. Maybe I see things out of proportion, or things that
aren't even there. Maybe I just don't know how to express what I feel. Who knows? You tell me, Babe.
You're my Doctor. . . .

"Anyway, I always felt the front office and the manager and the players should be one big family. They
shouldn't take sides against each other. Man, you live
part of your life with these people. They are, in a sense,
your family. The owner should be like a father to you,
take care of you, protect you. Take my last year at Cin-
cinnati [1970]. Everybody knew I was on the way out.
So why didn't the bastards start me one game, just one
last game? Why couldn't they let me go out in style
instead of letting me rot on the bench? Or the Angels.
The fucking Angels! They had an old-timers' game recently and they didn't even invite me. I wouldn't have
gone if they did, but Jesus, Babe, they've got my glove
and spikes in their Hall of Fame! I pitched the first
no-hitter in California major league history! I did it before Koufax or Marichal or any of those fuckers."

Bonnie, who has finished her toenails, stands up suddenly and yawns. She looks down at her toes and wig-

gles them. "How do they look, Bo?" she says. Belinsky looks at her, open-mouthed, stunned. "What, Babe?"

"My toes, Bo! How do they look?" She wiggles them again.

Belinsky shakes his head wearily and then smiles. "Babe, they look beautiful. Really beautiful."

Bonnie, satisfied, looks around the room, sighs and says, "Bo, there's nothing to do. I'm bored."

"Why don't you read a book, Babe?"

"Oh, Bo, I can't stand still long enough to read a book. Maybe I should go swimming."

"Sure, Babe, that's it." Then he points to the painter and adds in a whisper, "Go topless. It'll freak him out."

Bonnie purses her lips and says, "Bo, you're terrible!" She walks out of the room, her hands contorted behind her back unhooking the top of her bikini.

"She's some chickie, isn't she?" says Belinsky. "All she needs is a little silicone and I'll have to call up Heff." He laughs. "About a ton of silicone." He sinks back into his chair and begins cracking his knuckles. He is staring straight ahead at the chimney, which he seems not to see. His eyes pass through and beyond a picture of Len in a full-faced beard. Len's picture is superimposed over a poem that reads: "The drifter has vanished/The dreamer, with age, has gone blind."

Belinsky turns suddenly and leans over the arm of his chair, the room reflected in concave miniature in his dark glasses. "You know, I played 15 years of baseball and never made a dime off it. I wasn't that interested in success, that's why. I loved the game, Babe, not success. Most ballplayers are whores at heart. Do you think Seaver or Ken Harrelson play the game because they love it? You bet your ass they don't. They love what it brings them, Babe. I could never give up enough of myself for success.

"Len Schecter approached me about a baseball exposé long before he ever hooked onto Jim Bouton. I told him I wasn't interested. I couldn't rat on guys I'd played with, even if they were bastards. That's not my style. I was the last of baseball's true sportsmen. My heart was in the game—the game, the fucking game, that's all. I never stashed baseball. You know what I mean? Stash! Stash! Stash!" He stands up and thrusts his hand down his leg as if into his pants pocket. He repeats the gesture again, again, again, while saying, "You can't stash 'sport.' Those other bastards talk about 'sport' and they mean 'business,' they mean something they can stash in their pockets. Man, you can't stash baseball. If you're lucky, you capture it awhile, you go through it at some point in your life and then it goes away and you go on to something else. Some guys try to live off it forever. Babe, it's a sin to live off 'sport.' "

Belinsky sits down again. He is quiet for a moment, trying to compose himself. Then he says softly, but in measured tones, "I mean, baseball is a beautiful thing. It's clean. It stays the same. It's an equalizer. It moves slowly in a time when everything around us is rushing like mad. It's a . . . gee, what am I trying to say. It's a breath of fresh air blowing across the country. Don't laugh, I mean it! Listen, during World War II when those Jap kamikaze pilots flew down the smokestacks of our ships, do you know what they screamed? 'Fuck Babe Ruth!' That's right, 'Fuck Babe Ruth!' Not 'Fuck Knute Rockne!' or 'Fuck Bronco Nagurski!' but 'Fuck Babe Ruth!' That's the way I feel about the game, even today. I just never knew how to express myself properly, that's all. I loved the game, but I love it my way, not the way people told me I should love it.

"I owe baseball. It kept me straight. Who knows what I might have been without it. Baseball was the one big thing in my life—if my life contained any big thing. My running around with broads, that was just passing time. It was baseball that mattered. I mean, Sport keeps you clean, but only for a while. In the long run it isn't even Sport that matters, it's you. You've got to know when to get off or else you start handing out too many transfers."

Belinsky reaches down for his glass, picks it up, then, without taking a sip, returns it to the table. "Take this house," he says with a sweeping gesture of his arm. "I'm just a guest here. No matter where I've been or who I've been with, I've always been just a guest. I like it that way. I'm like camouflage. I blend in anywhere—but not for too long. Pretty soon I think I'll head for the Islands. If I stand around here too long I'll kill the grass. That's the way I've set up my life. I don't want to take root anywhere. You hear about good soil here or there and you're curious, but really you're afraid to find it. I mean,

Babe, you take root, you give your trust to someone, and it's bound to fall apart. I don't want to be around when things fall apart. I'm more spiritual than people think. I don't do malice to anyone. I don't like to see people hurt. When I sense things are falling apart—I have this radar—I snap alert, and then I'm gone. Follow the sun, Babe. That's it, I follow the sun. . . . I hate it, this way I am. But who chooses to be what he is, huh? It's in the stars, Babe, in the stars. I would like to be devoted to someone or something. . . . I just never found anything I could lend myself to. The age of chivalry is dead, Babe. There are no more heroes."

He smiles and stands up. "Nothing left worthy of devotion, know what I mean? That's why my way is best. Don't forget, 'He who plays and runs away, lives to play some other day.' " He throws his head back and laughs, that self-mocking laugh. Then he holds up his empty glass and says, "Excuse me, Babe. I need more Wheaties. Besides, this conversation is getting a little heavy. Too heavy." He laughs again as he moves off. "Too heavy, Babe." He moves with a long and graceful stride, his body shifting delicately from side to side, his weight slightly forward on the balls of his feet. And yet he moves so lightly, ever so lightly, a man on hot coals, a cat about to spring or flee, leaving not the slightest indentation on this thick carpet over which he passes.

March 1972

The Winner Who
Walked Away

Philip Toll Hill is a forty-nine-year-old businessman
with a vivid, if selective, memory. He can recall the
make, model, color, year, and gearshift pattern of every
automobile he has ever been in, and he can visualize
minute details of every funeral he has attended. He remembers, for instance, that as an eight-year-old he and
some friends were driven home from a birthday party in
a green 1933 Chevrolet sedan whose gearshift had a
sloppy neutral and a spongy feeling when the gears were
changed. He remembers the feel of that gearshift because he was permitted to sit beside the driver and shift,
but only after he had paid each of his friends 25¢. His
friends laughed at him and, for the first time, he wondered if his fascination with the automobile might
somehow be unnatural. About the only things Hill can-

not remember from that childhood incident are the names of his friends and the driver.

Hill also remembers another moment, when, at twenty-four, he stood over a casket and scrutinized his mother's features. He grew disturbed, not from emotion but by her looks. He summoned the undertaker. "Those aren't my mother's lips," he said. "That is not the way they were." Then, in precise detail, he described how his mother had painted her lips so that the undertaker could repaint them.

For a good many years and almost to the exclusion of all else, Phil Hill's life was devoted to mastering automobiles and outwitting death. He has owned, driven, raced, and restored more automobiles, and he has attended more funerals, confronted and contemplated death more often than most men would in a dozen lifetimes.

Throughout the 1950s and early 1960s, Hill was the most successful American racing driver, and he remains the only American ever to win the World Driving Championship. He began his career as a mechanic for midget cars around his hometown of Santa Monica, California, graduated to driving an MG-TC roadster in 1947, won his first competitive event in Gardena in 1949, and his first major U.S. sports-car race in 1950 at Pebble Beach. He was twenty-three. He drove a new XK-120 Jaguar. It was long, low and hump-fendered, and as sleek as its namesake, but by the time Hill finished punishing it at Pebble Beach, it was merely another muddy, dented, brakeless, and clutchless racing hulk. Hill's driving technique at the time consisted of plowing his car into each turn too fast, bracing himself as the car bounced off the track's protective bales of hay, and then jerking the steering wheel until the car straightened out and proceeded to the next turn—with his foot nailed to the gas pedal. It was a technique that showed neither style nor fear, and one that would change.

Hill built a reputation as the premier sports-car racer in the States during the early 1950s and then went to Europe to enhance that reputation. Ultimately he became a Grand Prix driver for Enzo Ferrari. A Formula I car is the quickest, flimsiest, and most dangerous of all racing machines. Hill approached it with caution. As a Formula I driver, he was never the fastest in the world—that distinction belonged to Stirling Moss—but during the early 1960s he was the best. Whereas Moss had a talent for driving the fastest laps and sometimes even the fastest races, he also had a propensity for disastrous crashes and for punishing his car beyond its breaking point. He led a great many more races than he ever finished, while Hill, having learned discipline and restraint, finished an extraordinary 80% of the time. Hill was never in an accident for which he had to be hospitalized, nor did he have a reputation for breaking cars. He was a perfectionist, about cars and the tracks over which he drove. Before each race Hill toured the track in a sedan, slowly, stopping to pick up wet leaves. He made mental notes of every tree whose branches might drip morning moisture on the track, and of every building that might create crosswinds that would lighten his car at high speeds. He was equally fastidious about the preparation of his car. On the night before he won the world championship he forced his Ferrari mechanics to install a new engine simply because the existing one did not sound right.

Hill seemed to see things before they happened. While other drivers often found themselves in trouble and had to use every bit of their skill to extricate themselves, Hill anticipated such situations and avoided them. Intuition saved his life in 1955, when he was standing on a bench in the pits during the 24 Hours of Le Mans. "I had always worked out what I would do if a car got loose in the pits," Hill says. "When the cars came down the straightaway I heard this unfamiliar sound . . . pttt . . . pttt. I didn't think, I just jumped backward off the bench and crouched down." A Mercedes 300 SLR hurtled into the crowd at about 100 mph, killing 83 and injuring more than 150, and although Hill could see a gendarme lying nearby, legless, on the track, he was unscratched.

For years Hill accepted death as inevitable in his profession. When he signed on with Ferrari in 1956 he was the ninth driver on a nine-man team, but by the time he won his championship in 1961 four of those teammates had been killed in crashes. By the fall of 1961 most of the great Formula I drivers of the 1950s had been killed,

twenty of them in races in which Hill had been competing. Among the dead were his Ferrari teammates von
Trips, Hawthorn, Collins, Castellotti, Musso, Portago,
and others like Lewis-Evans, Behra, and Schell.

The death of von Trips most affected Hill's career
because it came in a fiery crash during the Grand Prix of
Italy, the race in which Hill cinched his championship.
Had von Trips lived, Hill might never have become
world champion, because at the time the German was
leading Hill for the title, 33 points to 29. This knowledge weighed heavily on Hill during the winter of 1961,
when he should have been savoring his title. He grew
obsessed with the attrition rate of his fellow drivers, and
with his own mortality.

Within three years Hill would leave Grand Prix racing
without approaching his 1961 success. He returned to
safer sports-car racing for a few years and then in 1967,
at the age of 40, left the sport altogether. His retirement
was not brought about by injury or by age, since many
racers drive through their forties. And Hill retained no
contact with his former profession. He gave up the
sport, he says, because "I had a premonition I was ultimately going to kill myself and, more than anything, I
did not want to be dead."

Today Hill lives with his wife and three children in an
old Spanish-Mediterranean-style house in a quiet
neighborhood in Santa Monica. The house is surrounded by newer homes, but when his parents bought
the place in 1929 it was one of only two houses on the

street. He has tried to preserve the house exactly as it was then—white plaster walls, exposed beams and dark wood floors. When he was a child the house was meticulously kept by servants, and the only brightness was the colorful mosaic tiles embedded in the stairwells leading to the second floor. Now the house is comfortably rumpled with his children's plastic toys and stuffed animals and highlighted with ancient objects of his own.

A perfectly restored violano lies under glass. An old Bible lies open on a book stand. Volumes with leather bindings and parchment pages edged in gilt are stacked in bookcases and propped on coffee tables. One wall from floor to ceiling is lined with faded cardboard boxes that contain the remnants of his once vast collection of player-piano rolls. Two perfectly restored player pianos stand side by side, their polished chestnut gleaming. The past is everywhere, in the smell of worn leather and in the burnished woods that lend each room the quality of an old, brown-tinted photograph.

Hill takes a slim volume from a shelf and props his bifocals on his nose. A multimillionaire, he is dressed in a plaid shirt and corduroy jeans. He has a creased and harried face, and yet, with tousled hair and small features, he resembles a boy. He looks slight, but he says, "I am not! I am 5' 10", an average height."

He holds the book at arm's length as he turns the pages. The pages rustle. The book is an heirloom from his paternal grandmother, whose Dutch ancestors settled in New York State in 1685. It dates from 1837 and

contains poems, stories, letters, exhortations, and draw-
ings. It is penned by a variety of hands in tiny, elaborate
script. "Can you imagine the time it must have taken?"
he says. "What kind of life enabled them to devote such
time to this?"

He replaces the volume and withdraws a piano roll,
inserting it into one of his pianos. The keys begin to
move and the room is filled with *The Enchanted Nymph*
as performed by composer Mischa Levitzki. Hill seems
less enthralled by the music than by the moving keys.
"A minor piece," he says. "Not one of his best. I got
interested in restoring player pianos only partly because
of the music. Mostly, I wanted it to seem as if the pianist
was right here in the room, playing just for me."

The only part of the house that has undergone al-
terations is the garage which, by now, almost entirely
devours the backyard in order to accommodate Hill's
restored automobiles. His collection has grown so large,
in fact, that he must quarter many of his cars in
neighbors' garages. Only the favorites remain at home.
Each one is restored to a state far superior to its original
one. There is a silver 1947 MG-TC, identical to the one
in which Hill captured his first trophy. There is also a
1931 Packard convertible coupe purchased from a film
star. "You've got to see it!" Hill says. "You'll love it! It
gives you such a feel for the 1930s." He leads the way,
moving on to his favorite, a 1912 Packard 30, blue
trimmed in gray, aglow with brass trim. He reaches inside to the dashboard and flicks on the head lamps.

There is an audible "poof" and a whisper of smoke as the gas-operated lamps ignite. The flames dance inside their glass cases. "It represents the end of an automotive era; it was the last year for the right-hand drive," he says.

He stops beside a black 1918 Packard Twin-Six Fleetwood town car. Hill has a particular fondness for this Packard because it is the first automobile he remembers, the one he believes sparked his passion for automobiles. As a youth during the Depression, he remembers driving it and also the humiliation he felt when he was taken to school in it by a chauffeur. He was given that car by his aunt, who owned it, and it has put in only 20,000 miles. During his racing years Hill purchased and restored old cars as a hobby, and after he left racing he and a partner, Ken Vaughn, turned the hobby into a lucrative business that they now operate out of a garage in downtown Santa Monica. The garage is clean and brightly lighted. The employees are young men except for the upholsterer, an elderly Italian with whom Hill invariably stops to pass time, always talking in the man's native language.

There are about a dozen cars in various states of restoration. Each job varies, but a typical restoration will take up to two years and cost more than $75,000. The restorers quote no estimates, relying instead on their customers' trust. In one corner sits a wine and buff 1931 Packard Club Sedan with 79,000 miles on its odometer and the nameplate of its original owner—Princess

Jacqueline de Broglie—attached to its walnut dashboard. The car, restored at a cost of $50,000 and two years of labor, is in a state so pristine that before it leaves the shop Hill, who does much of the work himself, will even wipe any dust from the engine. What is holding up the car's return to a local ophthalmologist is an almost inaudible squeak in the dashboard. "It should not be there!" cries Hill. If necessary he will dismantle the dashboard again to eliminate the squeak.

Near the '31 Packard is the stripped frame of a '27 Packard that has just been sprayed with purple enamel, its original color. Every screw and bolt and color in a Hill-restored car will match the original. Once, admiring an old car at an antique-car show, Hill noticed a screw that did not belong. He lost all interest in the vehicle. He will purchase parts at a junkyard, an auction or an antique-car show or, if necessary, will reproduce them in his own machine shop.

"My cars must be sound mechanically," says Hill. "First, they must run right, as they were intended to. I drive all my old cars. I have this acquisitive streak. I love to go to car shows and mill around among the bolts and nuts—the parts, not the people—and search for some old bumper. It's symbolic, as if by possessing a thing you have a certain distinction. My old-car passions have changed, though. I can go to another collector's house now and enjoy his belongings without envying them. Mostly, though, I restore old cars because it is what I do well. I get tremendous gratification from taking something in a decayed state and returning it to its former state. It's as if by restoring an old car I lived in another time and contributed to that time."

Hill is as inquisitive as he is acquisitive. In the past that inquisitiveness was directed toward the automobile, racing and, finally, death. Today, his curiosity shoots everywhere, to the serious as well as the trivial. He takes apart his wife's hair dryer simply to see how it works. He reads himself to sleep with medical books because he is curious about the mechanics of his body. Hill is committed to the principle that an unexamined life is not worth living. He often tries to understand himself by returning to his childhood. He flashes back, reconstructing in order to understand. Why, he wonders, did he devote so great a chunk of his life to racing, an endeavor he now calls "meaningless" and whose practitioners he characterizes as "insane."

In the 1930s, when most Americans were struggling, Hill's life was peopled with servants, chauffeurs, music tutors, and his indulgent aunt, who bought him a car when he was twelve. He was, however, deprived in less tangible ways. Like the offspring of many wealthy parents, he was overprotected. He was not permitted to play baseball or football—he still harbors a fear of catching a thrown ball—nor could he date girls as early as his less affluent contemporaries did. His mother, Lela Long Hill, was, according to Hill, an austere, pampered, and domineering woman who wrote and published religious hymns (*Jesus Is the Sweetest Name I Know*) and contributed money to evangelical crusades. Often she forced her son to stand with her for hours in the rear of a revival tent, listening to fiery admonitions. She was a contradictory woman, however, and in her youth was said to have had "a serious flirtation" with a famous Cleveland Indians baseball player, whose name the family has conveniently forgotten. Hill remembers his father only as a serious, unloving man whose advice on sending him off to military school was, "Be a good little soldier." His father also trained him to greet women with a bow and a click of his heels, a habit Hill retains, "a damned reflex!"

"It wasn't until the car thing that I felt any worth," Hill says. "I've always expressed myself via the automobile. I guess I sensed that I was in an insane environment and that my only escape was in something that had structure. Cars gave me a sense of worth. I could do something—drive—no one else my age could do. I could take cars apart too, and when I put the nuts and bolts back together again and the thing worked, no one could prove me wrong. That kind of technology was fathomable, made sense in a way people never did. Cars are easy to master; they hold no threat; and, if you're careful, they can't hurt you like people can. I have been a 'thing' person all my life."

Hill was the first of his age group to learn to drive, and when others followed he outstripped them again by his daring on the city streets and subsequently on the racetracks of Southern California. Without planning it, he became a sports-car racer simply to remain a step ahead of his contemporaries. "As a young racer I was a nut-case," says Hill. "My own worst enemy. I drove on instinct, not intellect. I would go out and go too fast and sort of scramble around making sure to react to danger rather than doing a heady job."

Hill had been sports-car racing for almost five years when, in 1953, he began to suffer stomach pains that were diagnosed as caused by an ulcer. He feels now that the ulcer was brought on by a suppressed realization that he was engaged in a deadly sport. Under doctor's orders he quit racing for a year until the trouble sub-sided and then returned, determined to pursue his career to its ultimate conclusion. By then he had be-come ambivalent toward a sport that he could do so well and enjoyed on an instinctive level but which, on an intellectual level, he increasingly began to see as de-structive.

His driving style changed drastically from one of reck-less instinct to one of meticulous discipline. He formu-lated the theory that a driver affects his odds to such a high degree that he could learn to drive on the edge of disaster without ever going over that line.

By 1961 Hill's anxieties surfaced dramatically when, after the depletion of Ferrari's Formula I ranks through fatal racing accidents, he and Count Wolfgang von Trips found themselves the drivers with the best chance to win the world title. Hill became obsessed with winning it, partly from an urge to excel, and partly from a desire to get approval from Enzo Ferrari, whom he described as "a hard bastard whose ambition in life was to build the greatest racing machine," and yet "a man I respected and from whom I wanted more than anything affection and for him to be a good daddy."

Hill's relationship with *Il Commendatore* was every bit as charged as the one he had had with his own father. Hill was repulsed by Ferrari's "pompous, patrician superiority" so similar to his father's and by Ferrari's attitude toward his drivers. "To this day I do not know if he had any genuine feelings for us as individuals," says Hill, "or whether we were just tools tolerated as necessary evils. When one of us did win, it was more as if Ferrari felt the victory was doubly his—he had not only managed to build the fastest car but one that was good enough to foil his drivers' destructiveness."

To some degree, almost every driver in the Ferrari stable saw their leader as a father figure. Ferrari sensed this, cultivated it, and used it to push the men to greater efforts. The results were sometimes tragic. Says Hill, "There was something about the mood at Ferrari that did seem to spur drivers to their deaths. Perhaps it was the intense sibling rivalry Ferrari fostered, his failure to rank drivers and his fickleness with favorites. Luigi Musso died at Rheims striving to protect his fair-haired-boy status against the encroaching popularity of the Englishers, Peter Collins and Mike Hawthorn. And Collins, a favorite while living in the hotel within earshot of the factory, began to get a Ferrari cold shoulder when he got married and went to live on a boat in Monte Carlo. He was dead within the year. Time and again I felt myself bristling as Ferrari used Richie Ginther and Dan Gurney to needle me. And certainly Trips and I were locked in combat."

Ferrari fueled the rivalry between von Trips and Hill by refusing to name either as team captain during the 1961 season. He merely sat back and watched them fight it out for the championship that, in either case, would be his. Von Trips, the archetypical playboy-racer, was famous for a driving style as careless as his life-style. His compatriots called him "Count von Crash." Hill, however, was as disciplined and cautious on the track as he was off it. He talked about his fear of dying, a subject taboo among drivers. His fellow drivers dubbed him "Hamlet in a helmet." "I'm not sure I wasn't deliberately antagonistic," says Hill. "It was like my growing interest in piano rolls. I immersed myself in them so they would take away concentration from racing and prepare me for quitting. It was the same with my colleagues. I was painting myself into a corner with them and their attitudes so I would be forced into an action—quitting."

On September 10, 1961, at the start of the Grand Prix of Italy, von Trips had his four-point lead over Hill for the championship. Midway through the second lap, von Trips tried to pass Jimmy Clark at 150 mph, nudged Clark's car with his own, and plunged out of control into the crowd. Fourteen spectators were killed, as was von Trips. Still on the circuit, Hill was aware of the crash but ignorant of its extent, so he continued to drive an almost flawless race to victory and the world championship.

"My defenses were equal to the shock of his death," says Hill. "They were strained to the utmost, however, by the funeral. There were three services. The first was held in the Trips' castle near Cologne. A funeral mass was said and then a procession formed outside. It was raining, yet none of us wore raincoats or carried umbrellas. We walked a mile to the Trips' church. The pace was set by an old, old woman, dressed in black and carrying a symbolic brass lantern. There was a band, also dressed in black, which played Chopin's *Funeral March*. The casket was carried on Trips' personal Ferrari, an open model. It, of course, had to be driven very slowly.

"At the church another mass took place—this one was sung. Then the procession re-formed to go to the cemetery, perhaps another mile away. It was raining harder. The Trips' family chapel is situated on a knoll in the cemetery. The procession stopped at the foot of the knoll, eight of us clambered up the rise, slipping and sliding in the mud with the heavy casket. The last service was held and poor Trips was finally entombed. I have never experienced anything so mournful as that day."

During the first five years of his retirement Hill lived the kind of reclusive life to which he had grown accustomed during bachelorhood. Except for a maid and manservant, he was alone. Each day began like the one before. His manservant, Coakley, would knock on the bedroom door and, without waiting for a response, enter carrying a tea service. Coakley would deposit the tea service on the table beside the bed in which Hill slept. Oblivious to his sleeping master, Coakley would say "Good morning" and move to the window. He would fling apart the curtains, at which sound Hill would open a malevolent eye. Coakley would look out at the morning, sigh, and no matter what the weather—sun or smog—make the same response, "Well, Master, another dull day," and depart.

If Hill's life was no longer as stimulating as before, it was not dull. He immersed himself in activities. Some, like his piano rolls and antique cars, he had pursued while racing; others he had come to later. He undertook vigorous routines of weight lifting and calisthenics. He became an omnivorous reader of everything from medical books to *East of Eden* to articles on extrasensory perception, heredity, and the continuity of human experience. He formulated labyrinthine theories on such topics as sleep ("An impossible reconciliation can exist in one's mind that amazingly can be smoothed over by sleep") and life ("a continual bleeding off of frustrations") and, naturally, death. He decided that death was a transcendence to a new state in which the dead become part of the cosmic unity of all creation, past, present, and future.

Hill's most fascinating new toy was introspection. He used it unsparingly on himself in the hope that with enough time and distance, he would understand his past and his obsession with racing.

"If racers have one thing in common," Hill says, "it is a blind compulsion to race that transcends everything else. Such a man is turned on by the possibility that he is doing something that could kill him. It's an outlet for people whose lives and selves were inadequate. They try to put order and meaning into their lives by imposing their will on something potentially chaotic. A racer believes he makes his deadly machine safe. He plays God. He is one of the Blessed. His sport *must* be deadly so that in competing and surviving his skill takes on mystical qualities. The best way to anger a racer is to tell him his skill is just reflexes, eyes, an ability to see at 100 frames per second while the rest of humanity sees at 50 frames. They don't want to hear that. They want to hear that they are mutations, that they have a mystical gift transcending anything other mortals have. They prove they are blessed by surviving the ultimate challenge. It elevates them. The cliché is that racers have a death wish. Nothing could be further from the truth. They don't want to die, they just want the *possibility* of death. It's their way of reaffirming life, *their* life. Of course, the best way to reaffirm life is not to race at all. I couldn't say that until I quit."

On June 5, 1971, Philip Toll Hill married Alma Varanowski, a thirty-three-year-old California divorcée who had an eleven-year-old daughter. At the time of his marriage the bridegroom was forty-four years old and a previously confirmed bachelor with a manservant who would shortly be given his notice. "I never thought I'd get married," says Hill. "I had seen what happened to my parents."

Hill's decision was influenced by an incident at once familiar to Hill and yet so different from any he had experienced. "Alma's father had died," says Hill, "and they had the funeral in their house in Phoenix. They had been displaced persons during World War II, and had fled Germany and the Nazis to settle in Arizona. They lived a kind of pioneer life. Her father, who worked as a laborer, built his small house with his own hands. You could see where he added a room here, and later, a bathroom there. It was a simple, beautiful house. At the funeral Alma's mother sat by her husband's casket while mourners passed by. They were mostly these big, truck-driver types who'd worked with her husband. They were crying and *she* was consoling *them*. She hugged and kissed these guys and, I remember, amid the tears there was laughter. She threw her arms around me and kissed me and I kissed her. I couldn't believe I did it! It was something I would never do. My family did not touch, never expressed affection like that. But here is the thing I will never forget. The casket was open and she was sitting beside it. You could see him lying there as if he were sleeping, and all the while she was greeting mourners she was absentmindedly stroking his forehead, soothing him in a way I will never forget."

Alma Hill, a striking blonde with a hearty, expansive nature, says, "Marriage was quite traumatic for Philip. After all those years! When Derek was born, Philip decided that the house had gotten too small and so he was going to sell his piano rolls. He didn't have to sell them. It seemed to be a symbolic thing."

"I had spent years acquiring them," says Hill. "I had the finest collection in the world, but when the baby came I impulsively sold them. I catalogued them for the new owner and one night I got this terrible panic. It was like racing—I was painting myself into a corner so I couldn't go back."

"I cried when he sold them," says Alma. "He was deliberately giving up a part of his life for us."

"All my life I have been a 'thing' person," says Hill. "My wife is a 'people' person. I have been learning from her."

"I look at those old pictures of my husband," says Alma, "and he looks so different now. Other racers, the ones that remained in racing, look the same. Oh, they look older, but basically you can recognize them because they are the same person. Philip is not. He has undergone a psychic change that has changed the way he looks. My husband has worked very hard to remake himself into another person. But in some ways he can't. He would never be able to divorce himself from guys like Dan Gurney and Graham Hill, or move from this house and his cars. My mother had a saying: 'No matter what, you cannot cut blood.'"

Whenever Phil Hill was with Graham Hill, he addressed his friend as *"Due Volte Campione"* (two-time World Champion), while referring to himself as *"Una Volta Campione."* Graham delighted in such deference, but sensed something was amiss from the faintly mocking tone of condescension.

Hill would be the first to admit that on an objective level he has a distaste for the attitudes and pursuits of racing men. He fears that he may have lost some respect over the years by the ferocity with which he has lashed out against racing. He now seems intent on restoring his image. He goes to races again. He circulates among race people, around whom he is deferential, as if consigned to a purgatory of *mea culpas* for past transgressions. They view him warily, as a curiosity whose behavior cannot be predicted. "I wonder what brings old Phil out of the woodwork," they think.

Ironically, Hill has again become proud of his racing achievements. Now, secure, he accepts them for what they were. He realizes that no matter what he wills himself to believe, or to be, there will always be a part of him he cannot deny. He will never excise that part, only make his peace with it.

September 28, 1975, a blazing Sunday afternoon in Long Beach, California. Phil Hill, Dan Gurney and Graham Hill are sitting in Gurney's pickup truck as it eases through a throng of spectators. Here are three of racing's most famous retirees. They are wearing metallic racing suits. Their helmets rest on their laps. Occasionally they wave at their fans as they make their way to Ocean Boulevard, the starting line for the race course laid out through the city streets. There, 30,000 fans and three identical Toyota sedans are waiting for them. They have agreed to a three-lap match race in those Toyotas as a promotional gimmick before the first running of the Long Beach Grand Prix for Formula 5000 cars.

Only Phil seems apprehensive. Dan, now a car builder, appears less preoccupied with racing his Toyota than with the F5000 car he has entered in the LBGP. Graham seems merely distracted.

"I asked the Toyota mechanic if he bled the brakes," says Phil. "He says, 'Don't worry, they should last three laps.' I started screaming, 'What the hell does that mean? I'm driving the goddamned thing! Guys have got killed in this type of thing!' "

Gurney laughs. "Come on, Phil. Remember what Ferrari used to say? 'Not to worry. You get in, you drive, you win.' "

"But I don't want to win," says Phil. "I just don't want to stuff it and make an ass of myself. I should never have agreed to this."

"Well, why did you?" says Dan.

"I'll be damned if I know. . . . I only know we're gonna make fools of ourselves."

"Just one more time, Philip, that is all," Graham says.

"Oh, it's all right for you to say, Graham. You've only been retired a few months, and Dan's been *practicing* at Riverside! I'm an old man."

"Oh, Philip, you are not an old man," says Graham. "You are an old lady. You are an old lady exactly as you were years ago."

"Yes, I am," says Phil. "I haven't changed, Graham, and I'm proud of it."

When they reach the starting line, jammed with spectators, Graham says, "Well, chaps, I am simply going to put on my helmet, crawl out on all fours and hide behind a tire." The truck stops, and they get out to thunderous applause and the flashes of dozens of cameras. Gurney is the favorite. He turns, smiling, to wave at the shouts of his name. Graham poses for a pretty woman photographer who coos, "He's such a dreamboat!" Phil signs autographs on the back of LBGP programs that carry a biography of him. He says, "Graham, will you look at this! It mentions how I finished third at Monaco in 1961! I finished SECOND in 1962! Why the hell didn't they mention *that?*"

They pose for one last picture, standing side by side with their arms around each other's shoulders. Phil, in the middle, is dwarfed by the other two, each over six feet. Their racing suits are sleek-fitting while his is old-fashioned and baggy as if he has shrunk and no longer has the stature of the man who once wore it. The photographer asks them to put on their helmets. The helmets of Gurney and Graham Hill have dark Plexiglas spaceman visors that cover their faces. Phil's helmet looks like a beekeeper's hat. It has a small peak and a colorless Plexiglas visor that only covers his eyes. Inside the helmet is printed: "Herbert Johnson, 39 New Bond Street, London, West. By appointment hatters to the late King George VI."

The picture taken, they get into the Toyotas. They start the cars, whose open exhausts sound, according to Phil, "like a flatulent cow. What I wouldn't give for the sound of a Ferrari now."

The race is uneventful. Phil's fears are unfounded as all three conspire to cross the finish line together. When they return to the starting line, the F5000 cars are staggered on the grid. The three retired drivers emerge from their Toyotas and are given a brief cheer, but already the spectators' attention has turned to the sleek racing cars that will reach upwards of 175 mph through the city streets.

Gurney hurries to his F5000 car and crouches down to give his driver, Vern Schuppan, advice. Graham Hill vanishes. Phil Hill begins the long walk back to the paddock area. He is sweating and agitated as he walks, the F5000 cars on his left and the spectators, behind a wire fence, on his right. Occasionally, someone points him out and calls his name; the phrase "world champion" can be heard. Hill is oblivious to all. He is walking very fast and talking. "Well, I'm glad that's over. I wasn't kidding! You could get killed in this type of thing. I remember Mike Hawthorn. He was on his way to an awards dinner and his car hit a tree. He was killed instantly. He had only been retired for a couple of months!"

Hill is walking past car after car on the grid. The drivers, encased in their cockpits, are all perfectly still. Their hands are stretched out before them, gripping tiny steering wheels. They stare ahead, mindless of the mechanics hovering near them.

"It's just like I thought," says Hill. "It's the kind of thing you don't want to do. I could never just race a little. It's like an alcoholic taking one drink. It's possible to rid oneself of the psychopathic aspects of drinking and drink normally again, but it's not worth the chance." Hill's voice is strangely loud now, because suddenly there is silence. The spectators are standing, their attention directed to the start. A man in a powder-blue blazer and white slacks is walking between the race cars toward the first one on the grid, carrying the starting flag.

"It's like when I went to Europe," says Hill, his voice growing still louder. "I had been married only a few months when I went over to be with the guys. I lived a bachelor life again, and when I came back to Alma, all of a sudden I couldn't sleep. I had the shakes, this terrible panic that I was really married and it was all over. Who the hell wants to go 55 mph for the rest of his life?"

Hill is alongside the first car on the grid now but he does not even notice it or its driver, Tony Brise, a

twenty-three-year-old Englishman who is the protégé of
Graham Hill. Two months later Tony Brise will be sitting alongside Graham Hill in his light airplane when it
crashes on a golf course outside of London, killing them
both.

March 1976

A Clutch of Odd Birds

Joe McNeill's mother used to say there's a Mort Berger in every town, and she may have been right. But those of us who knew him in the summer of 1962 liked to think she was wrong and secretly hoped he was unique. Berger was the proprietor of the only pool hall I can ever remember seeing in our small town in Fairfield County, Connecticut. He was a Jew from South Philadelphia who spoke out of the side of his mouth. On windy days he stuck bobby pins in his hair, which was deep reddish brown, the color of an Irish setter's. But, at thirty-three, he didn't have much to stick bobby pins in. To compensate, Berger let the little patch of hair at the base of his neck grow until it would reach far down his back if he let it—which he didn't. Instead, he combed it forward over his brow where he teased it into a tuft like a rooster's comb. Actually, Berger resembled a rooster more than anything. He had watery blue eyes, a pointy nose, and the gently curving, bottom-heavy build of a Rhode Island Red. He waddled.

Berger's greatest fear was that a strong wind might come along and reveal his artifice. To defend against this possibility he ventured outside the pool hall as infrequently as possible. This tended to make his pale and mottled redhead's skin so opaque that veins were visible beneath it. Whenever he did appear outside he walked about with his hand flattened over the top of his head like a man who had misplaced a migraine. Finally, in desperation, he had resorted to bobby pins. It was hard for anyone, at first, to talk casually to Berger without breaking up at the sight of the bobby pins, but after a few withering looks one learned to ignore them. The only person I ever heard question Berger about them was a college freshman who wandered into the pool hall one day, challenged Jack the Rat to a game of dollar nine ball, and then, pointing to Berger's hair, asked, "How come you got bobby pins in your head?" The place fell mute. It seemed even the skidding billiard balls froze in midflight. Berger's face took on the color of his tuft. He fixed a beady-eyed stare on the offender and said in a voice the recollection of which still sends shivers down my spine, "You, my friend, are banished for life." The humiliation! Worse even than Kant's categorical imperative! It would have been better for the boob if Berger, yarmulke over his tuft, prayer shawl about his shoulders, had intoned the Hebrew prayers for the dead.

That moment left a deep impression on all who witnessed it. Berger had banished most of us at one time or other, for offenses like firing a cue ball through a plate-glass window, or breaking a cue stick over the head of a $20 loser who promised he would return the next day with the money, but never for life. The worst we had ever received were indeterminate banishments such as, "until Jack the Rat returns with coffee." But a lifetime banishment! That went contrary to the one, all-abiding dictum with which Berger governed his life: "Never bounce a potential turkey." To have broken that golden rule without the slightest hesitation forced us all to view Mort Berger in a more spiritual light. He became for us, from that moment on, a man of principle.

Berger's ambition almost from childhood was to become a hustler—cards, pool, horses, craps, etc.—so that eventually he could fulfill his dream of owning a combination bowling alley and pool hall that would cater only to families and young couples. "A place with class," he liked to say. It must have occurred to Berger somewhere along the way that Philadelphia was too large a city for his modest talents, and so he began shopping about for a nice suburban community where his meager ability would be magnified by the citizenry's naiveté. He would content himself with being a big fish in a small pond or, rather, a big rooster in a small henhouse. That was why, in the spring of 1962, Mort Berger turned up

in the quiet Fairfield County community. It was an affluent and virginal suburb of New York City, ripe for
Morty's talents.

Berger promptly opened The Golden Stick in a neat
boxlike building out on the Boston Post Road. The day
before the opening he was confronted by a delegation of
the town's teen-age wastrels. The group included Jack
the Rat, Speedo, The Rodent, Len the Worm, and
Hank. Berger, perched high on a ladder outside The
Stick, was swathed in white overalls and had a
paintbrush in his hand. He warned the delegation below
that The Stick would be "a place with class." Then he
added, shaking his paintbrush in a menacing manner,
"No trash is gonna be allowed inside." Looking up,
Speedo was splattered with orange paint. The boys nodded at the warning and departed.

For a while Berger seemed to make an effort to be
faithful to his word. The Stick did not look like one of
those musty, nefarious pool halls that can be found in
any big city. Outside it was painted that bright orange,
and within the walls were a soft powder blue. There was
a gold carpet on the floor. Berger's small office was
paneled in pine and had a half-door that allowed him to
follow the action around the room. The pool tables were
new Brunswick models with felts of orange, gold, blue,
and the more traditional green. Hanging from the walls
were dozens of cue sticks and an assortment of placards
that warned The Stick's patrons the management would
tolerate no profanity, no gambling, and no minors. A

minor was defined eventually as someone who had no money and/or was still being breast-fed.

On the first few days Berger stood in the doorway of The Stick, resplendent in a brown blazer with a crest of grapevines on the breast pocket, and handed out orange membership cards for the sum of $1. Nobody could enter without one. The card informed the bearer that he was entitled to all the privileges of The Stick. Berger (or rather "the management," as he liked to refer to himself) reserved the right to revoke those privileges at any time and for any reason. Today the membership cards are considered something of a collector's item in Fairfield County. Their holders are a parochial lot, often referring to one another (much as the survivors of a great battle might) as the "originals." The originals still meet once a year, making a pilgrimage to Philadelphia, where today Mort Berger is the proud owner of his combination bowling alley and pool hall. Joe McNeill, who purchased the first membership card, had it laminated recently.

Although Berger might honestly have conceived of The Stick as a place with class, it did not take long before it became, in fact, a hangout for the town's high school and college students, fledgling pool sharks fresh from seven viewings of *The Hustler* and assorted "trash" between the ages of fifteen and twenty-five. Day or night one could find games of stud poker, nine ball, and Chicago; baseball, basketball, and football betting slips; racing programs and forms from Roosevelt and

Aqueduct; and three small shells under which Mort Berger would gladly place a bean that would magically disappear the moment you slapped down a dollar bill. Berger did not need a house to fall on his tuft before he realized that his conception of what The Stick should be had to be altered drastically. He stopped wearing his blazer, threw away his membership cards, rolled up his sleeves, and became The Stick's chief organizer of any and all games of chance.

As a result, The Stick became crowded and boisterous, so filled with the sounds of laughter, anger, profanity, and anguish that it seemed always on the verge of destroying itself with its own pent-up energy. The place was dominated by the regulars, who stood conspicuously against the walls, Knights of the Cue Stick leaning on their foils, waiting faithfully for the approach of a turkey. When one stepped through the door there was a barely audible "gobble, gobble, gobble" around the room before someone pounced on him. The turkeys seemed to enjoy the attention they received as much as anyone. It gave some of them a sense of importance, a recognition they probably would receive nowhere else in life. The $10 or $15 they lost daily was small price to pay for the solicitous and faithful attention of such a hustler as Speedo.

"Kwasi, where ya been? I thought you had died on me or somethin'."

"Naw, just a little cold."

"Thank God! You had me worried, Kwasi. You gotta

take care of yourself, kid. Think of your friends, the people who count on you. You know, Kwasi, you can't be recklessly selfish with so many people worrying about you."

"I guess you're right, Speedo."

"Sure I am. . . . Shoot a little nine ball, Kwasi?"

"Come on Speedo, whaddya think, I'm stupid?"

"Kwasi, how unfair! Just a friendly game. I'll even spot you the nine ball."

"I wouldn't shoot you if you spotted me the eight and nine."

"How about the eight, nine, and break?"

"Eight, nine, and break? Naw, I shouldn't."

"But Kwasi, you can't just go away. I want you, baby, I need you!"

When the turkeys were rare on particular days, the regulars passed the time playing practical jokes on Berger. One day Len the Worm threw a cue ball through the television screen in front of which Berger was placidly watching the Preakness; on another day Hambone took Berger to lunch at the nearby greasy spoon and, as he casually tossed a dead rat on the grill, turned to Berger and said, "Medium or well?" And on still another day The Rodent, in frustration over a missed shot, javelined his cue stick through the front window, almost impaling a bleary-eyed Berger, who was returning from an all-night poker session.

It is hard to say just how Berger viewed these pranks. Invariably they resulted in temporary banishment for the perpetrators, but when the big Chicago game began in the early afternoon, the exiled were readmitted.

The daily center of attention was the Chicago game played on table No. 1. In Chicago the players shoot the balls in rotation—one, two, three, etc.—and are paid only when they sink the one, five, eight, ten, or fifteen balls, which are called "money balls." The player whose balls total the highest number of points also wins money.

The players in the game seldom varied, including Speedo, The Rodent, Len the Worm, Hank, Gary, Berger, and myself. Speedo was so slight and baby-faced that he looked more like a fifth-grader than a high school senior. No one would ever have taken him for the consummate pool shooter he was, and this more than anything helped him assemble a faithful gaggle of turkeys, who found it inconceivable that they should lose money "to that little squirt." Speedo acquired his nickname because of the speed with which he could divest turkeys of cash and because he shot pool without taking so much as a split second to sight his shot, a tactic he had learned form Mort Berger.

Speedo was Berger's greatest admirer. He considered the proprietor a hustler of artistic proportions and studied assiduously at Berger's knee, to which he barely reached. However, Speedo lost confidence in his mentor one day when he and Berger teamed up to play a pair of strangers in a very expensive Chicago game. Midway through the game Berger stole an eight ball from the opponents' rack and placed it in his and Speedo's rack. When this discrepancy was discovered by one of the strangers he brought it to Berger's attention by repeatedly poking the tip of his cue stick into Berger's chest. This left little blue chalk marks on Mort's white shirt and drops of perspiration on his brow. The chalk marks looked like bullet holes from a distance. Berger assumed his most smitten air—wide-eyed, open-mouthed, incredulously pointing a finger at himself—and turned to a confused Speedo and said, "Son, I told you never to do that. I run an honest game here. I have my reputation, you know."

If it were not for Berger's intervention the two strangers would have played chicken wishbone with Speedo's frail and trembling frame. As it was, they left contentedly after scooping up all his spare cash. As the door shut behind them Berger was heard whispering to Speedo, "I told you never to steal a money ball, Speedo. Steal the four or six if you need to. Nobody ever pays attention to a four or a six."

Len the Worm, another regular, was a dark, shifty-eyed youth who perpetually glanced over his shoulder as if expecting some fearful specter to tap him at any moment and lead him away to God only knew what torments. The Worm had an odd, shaky, clawlike bridge with a cue stick, and although he shot a decent enough game he seldom sank a money ball. His bridge hand would shake terribly. He would gulp in air, running his tongue over his dry and pursed lips as he bent over to sight a shot. Pool affected us all a little like that, I guess. It was more than just a game or a means to easy cash. It was for us a symbolic playing out of some inner turmoil. The confrontation was not with a $5 money ball but with something that ball represented for each of us, some inner and complex doubt we were unable to overcome in reality, but which could be momentarily mastered by the simple act of shooting a colored plastic ball into a leather-lined pocket. It always brought short-lived success. Those inner doubts remained, undiminished, and they would reappear the moment we stepped outside of The Stick into what we began to refer to as "the real world." For most of us at that time, however, success on the pool table was a satisfactory substitute. It was for Speedo, say, proof enough that despite his size and appearance he could exhibit as much tenacity and courage as any 225-pound football player.

But, alas, The Worm hadn't even that meager consolation. He was a thorough loser. And whenever he did miss an easy shot, the ball hanging precariously on the lip of a pocket but refusing to fall in, The Worm would turn to his audience, his eyes flitting in their sockets like ball bearings in an empty glass, and say: "It moved, it moved! The table moved. Did you see it?" He would grab Jack the Rat's sleeve and tug it until in the end Jack nodded tiredly in agreement. "It musta been a earthquake or somethin', Jack. It musta. Why does it always happen to me?"

The Worm was particularly susceptible to the ploys of

Mort Berger, who could be counted on to sneeze, squeakily chalk his stick, jingle coins in his pocket or make a sudden move as if to catch a falling cue stick, causing The Worm to miscue and send the cue ball squibbling past a money ball. The Worm became so conscious of Berger's presence that after a while Mort no longer had to make a move or a sound in order to throw off The Worm's shot.

The Rodent, so named because his face came to a point at his nose, was the worst pool shooter among us. But he could afford to be. He was immaculately dressed in Brooks Brothers button-downs and Lord Jeff crew necks and seemed to be in possession of a bank-roll large enough to sustain the heaviest losses in a Chicago game. The Rodent was very status conscious. He was always working on some plan that would propel him into the public limelight. In his Stick days he even went so far as to pay some of the regulars $10 a week just to let him hang around with them so he could learn to be "one of the boys," as he put it. The Rodent and his schemes (which included weekend trips to New York City to attend arty East Side parties where he could make himself known) were a source of amusement to The Stick regulars. However, The Rodent had the last laugh. He married a New York fashion model who earned about $200,000 a year and was five years older than The Rodent. As proof of his elevated status in life, The Rodent returned to Fairfield County one day, rustled up as many former Stick buddies as he could find, and carted them off to his $250,000 New Jersey estate. There he showed them his 20-room mansion, his servants and the chauffeur-driven limousine that transported him and his wife to New York City each morning. When his friends asked him just what he did for a living The Rodent looked incredulously at them and said, "You mean, work?" He chuckled. He said he was a sort of producer, although he never mentioned what sort. Then he showed them a few yellowing Leonard Lyons columns from the *New York Post* that read something like: "What handsome young Broadway producer was seen holding hands with what high-fashion model at Arthur until the wee hours of the morning?" It was hard for his friends to believe that the "handsome young Broadway producer" was The Rodent. In fact, to this day none of us can ever remember seeing or hearing of any play that he produced. Of course, to be fair, I have to admit that we always tended to think of him as "The Rodent," which surely wouldn't be how his name would appear in the credits, and so we might have missed it a few times.

I haven't seen The Rodent in almost eight years, but Hank saw him recently in Miami Beach. Hank told him I was writing a memoir about our days at The Stick, and The Rodent became hysterical. He pleaded with Hank to intercede with me. "Tell him not to use my real name," he said. "If my days at The Stick ever get publicized it'll ruin me. In New York they think I have class."

The Rodent knew that if I'd listen to anyone it would be Hank. In 1962 Hank was seventeen and considered the most well-balanced and intelligent habitue of The Stick. He shot a neat, precise, left-handed game of pool and was one of the few shooters I ever remember seeing whose game improved as the bets were raised. He was Berger's "houseman," a term that meant house champion. Hank spent most of his free time in The Stick, often cutting classes at the high school he attended in favor of drifting down to help Berger dust off the tables or empty the garbage in the morning. Those of us who thought about it could never understand why a person of Hank's caliber wasted his time at The Stick. We eventually discovered that he was having trouble both at school and at home. Finally one day he quit school, his parents threw him out of the house, and that morning when I arrived at The Stick I saw Hank curled up under a blanket sleeping on the No. 8 table. He continued to sleep in The Stick for the following few weeks, thanks to Berger's generosity. To repay Berger, Hank cleaned up in the morning and generally ran The Stick until the management arrived late in the morning.

The only other regular who shot pool as well as Hank was Gary, a slight, pale eighteen-year-old with lank blond hair and a face completely devoid of character. His was one of those smooth, fine-featured faces with thin lips and a nose so delicate it seemed to flutter when he breathed. Gary was neatly dressed at the time, his khaki pants pressed and his longish hair watered and combed to the side. He was quiet, almost unobtrusive, and hung back in the shadows, practicing for hours by himself on a corner table. Gary never really participated in much of anything at The Stick during the first few months but seemed satisfied just to observe the action and the life around him. One day he decided that his game had improved enough to challenge me at nine ball. He shot decently for a while but then suddenly, as the pressure mounted, his game disintegrated, and even his features seemed to crumble like a plaster mask that had been cracked all along but only now was showing the fissures. After that game, which he lost, he drifted back into the shadows, practicing daily and declining offers to play anyone for money. About a month later he challenged again. I almost didn't recognize him at first. His clothes were unkempt, his hair disheveled and his handsome face had become bloated and yellowish, much as that of a man in the final stages of dissipation. The glands in his neck were swollen and so was his belly. He had lost teeth, I noticed. We played nine ball for a while, and he was so silent that just to make conversation I asked how he'd been.

Without looking up from his shot he muttered, "I'm still alive, ain't I?" I laughed at this, but he didn't. I later learned that he was not making a wisecrack but stating a fact. He had an incurable disease that should have killed him a year before. That was what accounted for his altered appearance.

Gary beat me for $15 that second time I played him.

He played a ruthless game that almost frightened me. He opted for the riskiest shots and more often than not he made them. He eventually became, with Hank, the best "money shooter" in The Stick and, when I asked Hank what accounted for such a sudden change in his game, Hank said, "I guess shooting pool doesn't hold much pressure for someone who knows he should have died months ago."

I was the last of the regulars to arrive on the scene. I found The Stick one summer night after having spent eight hours lugging bricks and mortar up a scaffold for a mason. Inside the orange building I could hear the screech of chalked cue tips, the click of ivory balls, and the crash of dollar bills fluttering to the felt—and it was music to dulled spirits. I picked up some balls and began practicing on a corner table. My hands were stiff from carrying the cement buckets, making it difficult to form a bridge through which to put the cue stick. This difficulty of mine did not go unnoticed for long and, as I fumbled about the table, a slim youth ambled over. He leaned against the wall, arms folded, and watched as I smacked the balls about with indiscriminate haste. He took careful note of my cement-stained clothes and my callused fingers. In a matter of minutes, however, I felt my cramped fingers loosen, and the stick, which I had been handling with all the grace of a hod carrier, becoming, as it always did after some shots, an extension of my arm. I did not change my awkward bridge, however, or the manner in which I was punishing the billiard balls. I had spent many afternoons under conical lights in towns like Quincy, Kokomo, and Keokuk, and had sent many cue balls galloping across green felt cloth in search of a hiding nine ball. In minor league baseball towns most of the games are played at night, and there are few diversions for the ballplayers during the long summer afternoons. There are movies, limpid blondes with strange accents, and, usually, a pool hall. So I picked up pool then, as a diversion from my pitching. But as my pitching deteriorated, pool became, instead, something more.

"Shoot a little nine ball?" said the kid.

I looked up as if surprised. "For money?" I said.

"Why not?" he said with a weak smile.

"I don't know. I can't play nine ball very good."

"What kind of game can you play?"

"I don't know for sure. I haven't played much. . . ."

"Listen, I'll play any game you want," he said.

"Any game?"

"Any game."

"Chicago. Dollar a point. You spot me the six, nine and break." I smiled as I racked the balls.

Driving home later that evening I fingered the crumpled bills stuffed in my pocket. Fifteen dollars was almost as much money as I made with the mason in one day.

The following morning I put on my work clothes, grabbed my lunch bucket, kissed my wife, and drove directly to The Stick. I never lugged another brick for the mason and became instead a regular of Mort Berger's emporium. Like the others, I came partly to make some easy money. Mostly I came because the excitement and easy camaraderie helped me forget, for the time, an abortive baseball career. Outside the pool hall it would come back to me, troubling and confusing me, so I found myself spending as many hours as possible within the safe bowels of The Stick. When my wife asked where I was until all hours of the night, I told her I'd begun working overtime for the mason.

In recent years I have begun to wonder whether any of us would have spent so much time at The Stick were it not for Mort Berger. Without him The Stick would have been a dispirited place. Berger was the first adult to treat many of the regulars as equals. He introduced them to a thousand new delights: pill pool, jack-up, stud poker, Jack Daniel's whiskey, races at the Big A, and stag movies at his home. The fascination was not so much with those delights but with the manner in which they were presented. For example, Berger played pool disgracefully. He was always talking or dropping his stick when someone was shooting a money ball; he was always "accidentally" moving a money ball with his stomach or his shirt or his elbow so as to put it in a better position for his next shot; he was always stealing balls we'd made and sticking them in his rack, and generally cheating in so many ways, so outrageously, that much of our entertainment came from watching his antics and trying to catch him in some new ploy that would be the topic of our conversation for the rest of the day. To catch Berger cheating became a game with us. It gave proof of our emerging shrewdness, of our ability to know when we were being hustled.

And no one ever doubted for a moment that Mort Berger was hustling us all. We knew that he organized games of pool so as to get as many shooters as possible on a table and thus assure the management a decent day's income. We knew that he agreed to buy whiskey so that he could charge us a $1 "handling fee"; that he held the poker sessions at his home so he could take 25¢ out of every pot "just for the house, boys"; that he held the stag movies so he could charge an "entertainment fee" for a film whose images flickered and faded so frequently that none of us can remember seeing a single erotic act performed on his gray walls. In short, we knew Mort Berger was using us, but we did not mind paying. Most of us were not sure whether he liked us or simply considered us reliable sources for his own gains.

"Even when you thought Berger liked you," said Hank, his reliable houseman, "you were never quite certain. He would be glad to do little favors for you that always seemed to end up helping him more than you. But there was a point at which he drew the line. The day you asked him for money was the day you ceased to exist."

Soon a debate arose among us as to whether Berger was a fool, a fraud, or a genius. Most of the turkeys who lost money to him daily considered him a fool. They had no conception of the skill with which he manipulated them on the pool table. Hank and I felt Berger was more of a fraud than anything else, although we differed slightly as to just how harmless a fraud he truly was. Increasingly, I had begun to see Berger as a somewhat harmful influence on us, although I could never articulate my reasons for such a belief. Hank disagreed. "Who has Berger ever really hurt?" he would say, and I would be forced to admit that I could not cite as an example a single person, or any instance in which Berger had been truly destructive. We both did agree, however, that Berger was certainly not as shrewd as some of the more impressionable regulars, such as Speedo, believed. Speedo was Berger's Boswell. He attributed to Mort's slightest word or deed genius of the highest proportions. "Did you see that?" Speedo would whisper breathlessly as Berger miscued on an easy money-ball shot. "A brilliant move by Mort Berger," he would add, shaking his head in admiration. "Typical of him, though. Typical." And when the next shooter sank that same money ball and Berger was forced to dig into his pocket, Speedo would shrug confidently and say there was a hidden purpose behind Berger's miscue that the rest of us mere mortals could never hope to fathom. "You just wait and see," he would warn.

The principal reason for this confusion as to just who or what Mort Berger was could be attributed to the manner in which he tossed off maxims without the slightest explanation. He left them uncompleted, cloaked in mystery, little half-truths that seemed to mean more than they did. Berger left us to debate their significance without any hint as to whether they were deliberate stratagems or foolish accidents. By far the most mysterious advice he ever imparted to us emerged one day while he was regaling us with stories of the various pool halls he had frequented through the years. "If I learned one thing from those places," he said, "it was this." He paused dramatically. Speedo strained toward him as Berger continued. "Never shoot pool in a strange joint unless you go to the men's room first." And then he left us and went into his office.

"Now what do you think that is supposed to mean?" said Hank. We agreed it was an idiotic piece of advice. It was not until some time later that Hank and I learned to appreciate its hidden brilliance. We were playing in an expensive Chicago game with two beefy, unshaven adversaries in a strange pool hall in upper Fairfield County. We had already lost $10 apiece, although we had not had to pay a cent yet. It had been agreed to settle up at the end rather than after each game. "It would be too messy tossing dollar bills on the table after each game," said Hank. I agreed. Now the situation was becoming very messy, indeed. Hank missed a shot, cursed and then came over to me. "Let's get out of this game," he said. "We're not going to beat this guys."

"We can't quit," I said.

"Why not?" he said.

"Because I don't have any money," I said.

"Oh," he said faintly and collapsed on a stool. His arms went limp, and he was muttering to himself. "They'll kill us," he kept mumbling. "They'll kill us."

I told him not to worry and get worked up. I would think of something. "Like what?" he demanded.

Then I remembered Berger's mysterious advice. "I've got it! Is there a men's room in this place?" He pointed to a door. "Listen, I'm going in there in a minute and I'll climb out the window and head for the car. After I've been gone for about twenty seconds you follow me."

Hank brightened considerably, and then just as suddenly his brow was furrowed in gloom. "What if there's no window?" he said.

"I'll make one," I said, pointing to my cue stick. "If you hear some banging, just put on the jukebox."

There was no window, and the walls were too sturdy to bash with a cue stick. We were forced to return and continue the game, which we salvaged with a closing flourish that brought us even. Then we quit, but not before we vowed never in the future to doubt Mort Berger's wisdom.

Eventually I became thoroughly disenchanted with Berger and life at The Stick. There was a succession of small incidents, each of which compounded the previous until finally I believed Berger to be a truly harmful influence on us all. Because of the way he used us for his own gains, no matter how small they might be, we had taken it as a mark of distinction to be able to use each other in the same way. For example, when we saw how

easily Berger destroyed The Worm's pool game with his
little irritations, we all took a shot at The Worm in the
same way. We humiliated him, really, because in destroying his game we were actually bringing to the surface his moral weakness for everyone to see. Ostensibly,
we did this to win his money but I think subconsciously
it gave us pleasure to watch him twitch with the pain of
his inner torment. Our pleasure came from knowing
that we were his superiors, that we were made of sterner
stuff, that each one of us had the power to make him
squirm like bait on a hook, and so he became a
scapegoat through whom we reaffirmed our strength by
every day exposing his weakness.

It had also begun to occur to me that Berger was a
destructive influence on Hank. When Hank had been
thrown out of his home by his parents, Berger encour-
aged him to begin sleeping in The Stick. He helped
reinforce Hank's belief that his parents didn't understand him, rather than, as most adults would have done,
encourage Hank to seek a reconciliation. Berger was
thinking less of Hank's future or, rather, loss of future,
than of The Stick's immediate gain. I could imagine
Hank twenty years from then, his skin puffy and chalk-
gray, bending over a pool table to rack the balls or
sweeping the previous night's dust and cigarette butts
out the front door in the morning.

But these incidents in themselves would probably
never have disenchanted me completely if it were not
for my having been told of Gary's collapse. It had been

obvious that Gary's physical condition was deteriorating rapidly. His neck and stomach would be bloated horribly one day and deflated just as horribly the next. He had grown so weak that often he had trouble shooting a cue ball with any authority. One day while he was in a nine-ball game with Len the Worm, he had difficulty straightening up from the table after bending over for a shot. After another shot he fell over backward. He was fully conscious, lying on his back, his eyes wide but unseeing.

"It was a frightening look," said Joe McNeill. "Not a look of fear or pain or anything, but one of recognition, as if Gary was finally face to face with something that had eluded him all this time, and that now he had resigned himself to. Len, Speedo, and I helped him up. He said, 'I'd better go home.' We drove him there, and his mother met us at the door. She told us to help Gary over to the couch in the living room and then as we left she said, 'Thank you for bringing my son home.' He died two days later."

The day Joe McNeill told me that story was the last day I spent in The Stick. With Gary's death I finally realized that my existence there, and that of all the regulars, was self-defeating, that it led nowhere, serving only as an escape from problems that could never be solved as long as we shut ourselves up each day inside that room. I blamed Berger partly for Gary's death. Maybe not for his actual death, but for the way he had contributed to Gary's wasting of his life. I felt that if it had not been for Berger's hypnotic influence over Gary, he would have found a more gratifying way to spend his last days rather than spilling them out over a pool table trying to hustle Len the Worm out of a $5 bill that he would never be able to spend.

I left The Stick and enrolled in a nearby college, was graduated some five years later and became a high school English teacher. During my first year as a teacher I noticed a small story in the newspaper one day that told of the closing the The Stick. It had been shut following a raid by federal narcotics agents. By then, the late 1960s, drugs had swept into Fairfield County, and it did not surprise me that The Stick had become a hangout for the town's junkies. It seemed to be just the logical extension of a pattern of existence that had been set up years before by Mort Berger. I scanned the story for his name and the names of other regulars I had known but could find none. I did not know those arrested, and I wondered what had happened to Berger. Then I put the paper down and forgot about it.

Probably I would never have thought again of Mort Berger or The Stick if I hadn't run into Hank a year ago. While browsing in a bookstore in Bridgeport, I looked up to see Hank stacking books. He was recognizable even after seven years, heavier, but with the same furrowed, serious look about him, only now it did not seem so brooding and ill-fitting on a man of twenty-six. He recognized me also, and we began to reminisce. I told him that I was a teacher, and he said that he was in his third year of college. He had received his high school diploma while serving in the Air Force, and the government was paying for his college education. I asked him if he ever saw any of the other regulars these days. He said yes. Hambone was a certified public accountant who only occasionally drove down to the Big A to place a modest wager. Joe McNeill was engaged, and Speedo, of all people, was a responsible businessman with a wife and child. "And of course you know about The Rodent," he said with a smile. "I guess Mort Berger would be proud of him today.

The only regular who had not turned out well, he said, was The Worm. "He's a junkie with a very bad habit," Hank said.

"I could have figured that," I said. "I read how The Stick was raided for drugs a few years ago. It's a wonder all the regulars didn't end up like The Worm what with Berger to influence us."

"Oh, Berger wasn't the owner then," said Hank. "He'd gone back to Philly. When he left, the whole place fell apart. No one had any ambition to hustle pool anymore, so they just sat back and started taking dope. That's when I joined the Air Force. If Berger had been there maybe The Stick would never have seen any drugs."

I asked him what he meant, and he told me, "Berger would never have stood for any drugs in his place. It would have hurt business. Junkies don't shoot pool, it doesn't hold any interest for them. When Berger was there he gave us all a common interest. It wasn't much of an interest, hustling pool, but it was better than some of the things we could have been doing. At the time, most of those guys were in pretty bad shape. We were messed up and needed someone like Mort Berger to keep us above water. He kept us occupied just long enough for most of us to straighten out, and those that didn't, like The Worm, well, he held them up as long as he could and when he left they just sank to their own level, that's all. But without Berger he might have gone down a lot sooner, you can bet on that."

"And what about Gary?" I said. "How did Berger help him?"

"Gary, I almost forgot about him. I don't know, unless it was that without pool and Mort Berger, Gary wouldn't have had anything to make him want to get out of bed in the morning." And as Hank spoke, it fell so neatly into place, and I realized he was right. That Mort Berger had played an important part in my life, too, and I owed him not a small debt of gratitude.

"But I don't think that Mort Berger had any idea what he was doing for us," said Hank. "I don't think he could see that far ahead. In fact, if he ever heard us talking about him like this he'd probably say we were lunatics."

And he might be right.

August 1970

What Made Richie Run?

In the late summer of 1965, Richard William Connors, a sheetrocker from Bridgeport, Connecticut, left work early one day and drove to nearby Fairfield University where the New York Football Giants were holding pre-season workouts. Without the slightest hesitation, Connors leaped over the restraining ropes meant to separate spectators from players and approached Allie Sherman, who was standing on the sidelines. Before Sherman could speak, Connors said, "Mr. Sherman, my name is Dick Connors and it would be to your benefit to give me a tryout with the Giants." Without skipping a beat, Connors then told Sherman his background. He was twenty-three years old, a graduate of the University of Miami, and in perfect physical condition. "I've been preserved from injuries for the past four years," Connors said. "I've gone to bed every night at nine o'clock. I haven't touched a drop of liquor or eaten too much starchy food, and I can beat anyone you've got on this club."

While Connors spoke, Sherman stared at him curiously. Connors, at 6' and 200 pounds, did look in excellent physical condition. He was so thickly muscled he seemed about to burst from his gray T-shirt and Bermuda shorts. But somehow he did not look like an athlete. His black hair was short enough on top, but it was unusually long on the sides and slicked back into what had been known in the 1950s as a "D.A." Connors was also an exceptionally handsome man—his features were what a second-rate novelist might called "chiseled." His large, square-cut jaw jutted slightly forward with more than a hint of stubbornness. But Connors looked a little older than he claimed. The skin under his eyes was puffy and dark. His teeth were too perfect. The more closely one examined his face the more one noticed that what once might have been an untouched prettiness had been replaced by a shattered handsomeness, as if the face, like those of soldiers, had been destroyed and then painstakingly rebuilt, all the features the same as before only now not fitting quite so tightly, so naturally, but instead glued together with the cement of human experience.

When Connors finished his speech, Sherman was silent for a moment, and then, for reasons known only to himself, told Connors to report to the team physician for a physical examination.

"I was really high," says Connors today. "Higher than I'd ever been in my life—and I'd been pretty high at times. My heart was beating so fast I was afraid to see the doctor. He might think I was on something."

After only a few days of practice it was apparent that Connors, a linebacker and offensive end, was as physically talented if not more so than any player Sherman had. It was also apparent that he had little football playing experience. He made glaring mistakes. He blocked the wrong people. He beat his man with devastating moves and then ran to the wrong spot. When he ran to the right spot he dropped easy passes. He caught one pass with his nose and was almost knocked unconscious. Still, by sheer determination and tenacity, Connors survived the first cut—something a few All-Americans did not do. He was even accepted by the Giants' veteran players who admired his unbounded enthusiasm for the game. Shortly after the second cut, which Connors also survived, he noticed that those same veterans had begun to avoid him. When he sat down to eat at the training table, everyone got up and left. He said nothing and ate alone. He realized the players must have discovered that he, Dick Connors, was the man known throughout the Bridgeport area as Richie Connors. Richie Connors was almost thirty years old. He had been preserved for the last thirty-seven months, not at Miami University, but at Wethersfield State Penitentiary where he had been sent

by a judge who described him as "an incurable drug
addict, a thorn in the side of society who must be cut out
and put away."

Richie Connors was born on Halloween in 1936 in
Bridgeport, Connecticut, a large factory city whose out-
standing cultural event each summer is a festival dedicated to the memory of the great circus showman,
Phineas Taylor Barnum, who once said, "There's a
sucker born every minute."

Connors' father, an electrical technician for a vaude-
ville theater, deserted his mother before he was born.
Mrs. Connors supported herself and her son by working
as an usher, and later she managed a theater that fea-
tured baggy pants comedians and aging strippers. Yet,
Frances Hurley Connors—a strikingly beautiful
woman—enjoyed her work. She took pleasure in rising
late each morning and sitting for hours at her dressing
table making up her face for a day that began near noon
and ended close to midnight. "My mother was a very
beautiful, very aloof woman," says Connors. "She came
from a Boston Irish family that had always pampered
her. She tended to think of herself in a theatrical way
although she never did anything theatrical except try to
look like a star."

Connors inherited both his mother's good looks and
her tremendous ego. He too thought of himself as a star,
although with no father and an always-absent mother, he
was a star without an audience. Left to the care of aged

grandparents and an occasional aunt who praised his good looks and little else, he took to the city streets where he built a reputation as an athlete and a troublemaker. At the age of ten he appeared in Madison Square Garden where he led his 85-pound basketball team to victory in a game played between the halves of a college double-header. By eleven he had branched out from picking off passes to picking open parking meters with a screwdriver. One afternoon he stole a basketball from a downtown department store and made his escape dribbling between shoppers all the way up Main Street. At twelve he was thrown out of a parochial grammar school for defying a nun, and at thirteen his mother commited him to Junior Republic, a reform school for orphans and unruly boys in Litchfield, Connecticut. At Junior Republic he satisfied his thirst for attention by making up three years of grammar school in a half year, thus gaining recognition as the school's prize pupil. He also continued to excel in sports, especially football.

Connors graduated from Junior Republic with a glowing recommendation at the age of fifteen, and returned to Bridgeport where he entered Bullard-Havens technical school the following September. In his freshman year he was the school's most celebrated varsity athlete. He led the basketball team to the state tournament, only to be suspended. In his exuberance at winning the last regular-season game by one point, Connors threw the ball into the air at the sound of the buzzer. The referee tagged him with a technical foul that allowed the opposition to tie the game after it had supposedly ended, and eventually win it in overtime. The Bullard-Havens coach was so incensed he vowed Richie Connors would never play varsity sports again at the school, and he was true to his word. Without sports, Connors was frustrated. He began skipping classes, and early in his sophomore year he quit school altogether.

Eventually, Connors began playing basketball and football with the area's many semi-pro teams. Competing against tough clubs like the Holyoke (Mass.) Knights and the Franklin (Pa.) Miners, and against men eight and nine years older than himself, Connors more than held his own. He was sixteen years old, 6' tall, and weighed 190 pounds. He was the best all-around athlete in the city and probably the state, and yet he was virtually unknown since the local newspapers never publicized feats of the semi-pros in the same glossy way they did those of high school athletes. Connors' reputation, which had just begun to surface at Bullard-Havens the year before, then went underground. He became known solely by word-of-mouth, and only by men and boys truly knowledgeable about city sports. No matter how emblazoned the achievements of a high school star, they were invariably dimmed by Connors' shadow, by that inevitable voice amid the wellwishers saying, "Connors would murder him one-on-one."

That winter, after the end of the high school basketball season, a tournament was held at the North End Boys' Club in Bridgeport. It was a meaningless event, really nothing but a showcase for a 6′5″ All-State center from another part of the state. The center appeared for warm-ups looking magisterially aloof: blank-eyed, crew-cut, his sweatsocks of the purest white and rising, as if starched, all the way to his muscled calves where they terminated in three red rings—the school colors. His adversary for the center jump was Richie Connors. Connors, at sixteen, was two years younger and five inches shorter. His sweatsocks were wilted in a way that has only become fashionable with the advent of Pete Maravich. Even then Connors did not look like an athlete, but, with his slicked back D.A., more like some wild-eyed Teen Angel, some leather jacket hood who had been dragged from his chopper for this game because his teammates were short a man.

The first time the All-State center got the ball he moved across the key and began what sportswriters had called his "classic hook shot." Richie Connors climbed his back and smashed the ball into his face. The second time the All-State center began his classic hook shot Connors stole the ball so deftly that the center did not know it. He stood poised at the foul line, his right leg raised, and his right arm extended away from his body in exquisite form as he prepared to flip the ball that Richie Connors was now dribbling down court. The stunned fans watched in silence at first, then with small murmurs, and finally roars of approval as Connors crushed his opponent's ego as totally as Bobby Fisher does those of his chess opponents. Connors, relishing his underdog

role, played with a savage intensity that was both terrifying and electrifying. He held nothing in reserve. He
opted always for the risk: the blocked shot, the stolen
pass, the outrageous fake, the existential leap that left
him exposed to either cheers or ridicule. With each new
humiliation, his opponent grew more cautious, his
moves more deliberate, constricted, until finally at
game's end he was frozen at mid-court, immobilized by
Connor's wild-eyed presence.

But for Richie Connors, young, handsome, talented,
thinking of himself as "the cock of the walk," such
triumphs were too infrequent. Without school they
were sandwiched around too much dead time, and so,
like his mother, he began rising late each morning before drifting downtown to spend the slow city days
in pool halls or on streetcorners in front of news stores
and hotels, passing the time with other dropouts, men
older than himself, who had interests other than
sports.

"He had no first name," says Connors. "No last name
either. We just called him Murchie, Murchie-man.
'Murchie-man's got the goods,' we'd say. He was older
than I was, maybe twenty, twenty-one. He was from
Texas. He said he was from Texas. He was a greasy,
whiny little guy, the kind who could squeeze under a
door. Even though he didn't play any sports I thought he
was real cool with his 'Heh, man' talk. He used to say he
couldn't hit the side of a barn with a football, and then
he'd smile and add, 'But I can hit a vein a mile away.'

Who knew what he meant in 1953? I was only seventeen. But I found out one day. Jeez, it's not the kind of thing you like to reminisce about, but I could never forget that day. It was late July, about 4 P.M., and it was hot downtown. We were standing outside a news stand and Murchie says to me do I want to get high. I said, 'You know I can't buy no liquor in Bridgeport, Murchie-man, people know me.'

" 'I don't mean booze,' he said—God, I can hear him now, that whiny voice saying—'I don't mean booze, Richie, I mean horse.'

"I started laughing. 'What the hell you gonna do with a horse, Murchie-man? You ain't in Texas now. You gonna go riding down Main Street Bridgeport?'

" 'Come on, I'll show ya,' he said, and we walked up a hill to his car. He kept it right in the glove compartment in little glassine envelopes. In those days police weren't on the lookout for that stuff, it was too rare. He said you take it with needles. I told him I couldn't stick no needle in my arm. He said he'd show me an easier way, and he rolled a dollar bill into a funnel. 'You can snort it,' he said. I wasn't terrified of it then because I didn't even know what it was. I said, 'You sure this ain't bad stuff, Murchie-man?' and then I snorted some. I got sick at first and then I got high. A few days later I snorted again. Then every day. By the time the football season started I was shooting up once in the morning and once at night. One night before a game, I waited until the team went onto the field for calisthenics and then I shot up in the locker room. It was hard to get the needle in my arm with all those pads on but just as I did, one of my teammates walks in and sees me. His eyes almost fell out of his head. In those days drugs weren't an "in-type" thing. It was a disgrace, something only blacks did. Anyway, I played that first half higher than a kite. Everytime I bent over for a play I could see my teammate giving me a fishy look and I'd start to laugh. I must have been a real pussy cat that first half because the other team ran all their plays at me. But I came down hard at half time. I even got a little sick, and when I started the second half I was a tiger. The first time they ran a play at me I almost tore this poor guy's head off. When he finally did get up, he kept looking back at me as he walked to his huddle. He couldn't believe I was the same guy. He thought someone else had put on my uniform during half time."

Although Richie continued to play sports that year his performances deteriorated. His weight dropped from 190 to 175 pounds. He began spending more time with Murchie. He also learned that it had been no whim on Murchie's part to turn him on to drugs.

"He and his friends had run out of ways to get money," says Connors. "They had hocked everything they owned and borrowed from everyone they knew. Murchie had even dismantled his mother's bed and sold it while she was out working. They needed new blood—mine. But even if I'd known that, I'd probably still have gotten involved. I couldn't let anyone think

Richie Connors was chicken, could I? Besides, I wanted to be a part of that group. We were like the Three Musketeers and all that crap. We stole together; we copped together; we shot up together. We were fooling the world, which at the time was pretty easy since there were only 11 white junkies and 40 black ones in a city of 150,000. It was all so easy we had to make it look hard. We snuck around corners; barricaded cellar doors with oil burners; hid the stuff behind bricks in walls; we were real cute. I think we got a bigger kick out of that cops and robbers suspense than the drugs. But mostly it was the togetherness thing. We needed each other. One guy had a car, another had connections, we all had something the others could use. We even had a crippled guy in with us. He'd been crippled in a motorcycle accident and had become an addict when they gave him too much morphine to kill the pain. We went through his $30,000 insurance settlement in about a year. Finally, though, they needed me the most. It felt good too to know there was always someone would say, 'We gotta wait for Richie. We can't cop without Richie. Richie's got the guts.' I'd do things none of them would. I was the only guy who would go into the black sections of town to cop (buy) drugs. I was the only white guy the black pushers trusted, because they knew I wouldn't talk if I was arrested. One pusher liked me so much that on Christmas he put green and red Christmas tape on all the envelopes. It was his way of saying. 'Have a Merry Christmas.' "

Since illicit heroin was considerably "purer" in the 1950s than it is today, a five dollar "bag" would sustain a typical addict like Richie Connors for an entire day. (Today that same bag would cost twenty dollars.) At first it was not hard for Connors to turn over five dollars a day. He borrowed money from his athlete friends, his relatives, and when those sources were tapped, he began selling small items from around his house—clocks, silverware, knickknacks, and so on. One day he lugged his mother's washing machine up out of the cellar and wheeled it downtown to a pawn shop. As his home's saleable items dwindled, Richie began stealing loose bills and change from his grandfather. When his grandfather would come home from a night of heavy drinking he would toss his crumpled bills on the bureau and fall on the bed asleep. Richie was careful to steal just enough money so that when his grandfather woke the next morning he would think he had spent the missing money on the previous night's drinks. "Every morning when he counted that money he'd have a little smile on his face," says Connors. "He thought he was some helluva drinker."

When Richie Connors and his friends began stealing in earnest to support habits that had grown to thirty and forty dollars a day, he solidified his position as the group's most important member. He was an audacious sneak thief. He could lay bare an unattended cash register in seconds. He once robbed the same grocer seven times without that grocer's ever discovering he had been robbed. "I was careful to steal just a little money each time," says Connors, "so he wouldn't realize anything was missing. Of course stealing was easier in those days. People were less cynical. They weren't afraid to turn their back on you."

Even the city's policemen admired his daring and dexterity. One officer told Connors' mother that her son was the greatest sneak thief he had ever chased. "He's quick with his hands," said the officer. "He's got great instincts, and he can think on his feet quicker than any thief I ever saw. Too bad he doesn't play sports. He might have been a helluva linebacker."

"I no longer played any sports by then," says Connors. "I was down to 175 pounds and I had no interests but drugs. But that didn't bother me. I was still the star of the game, only now it was a different game."

At first Richie and his friends stole haphazardly whenever they came across an item—car, radio, watch—that was an easy mark. Once they stole a truckload of furniture when they saw the truck's driver go into a bar for a drink. Their haul required seven trips to a friend's apartment where they stored their loot. When they returned to the apartment the following morning to divide up the booty, their friend met them at the door with an anguished look. He told them his wife had been thanking him for the furniture ever since she woke up that morning and saw it. "Couldn't we just keep a few pieces?" he said to Connors.

"I wanted to kill the guy," says Connors. "By then we

were all getting pretty sick every morning. We knew we were addicts now and we were no longer 'cute.' We were real wise guys who would do just about anything for drugs. It was about then we decided we needed a daily plan to get money, so we went into the construction business by day and the gas station business by night."

Each morning after an eye-opening shot, Richie and his friends would dress in construction clothes and travel from one newly built but as yet unoccupied house to another, stripping each one of every bit of saleable copper pipe. Like piranhas they could strip a house in minutes. Once they ripped out copper water pipes while someone was taking a bath upstairs. When the bather yelled downstairs, Richie told him they were from the water company and then fled. When it grew dark they would all pile into Murchie's battered old Cadillac and drive toward New York City on the Old Boston Post Road. Along the way they stopped at every other gas station they came to. At each station Murchie would ask the attendant to check under the hood, while Richie would go inside the office, ostensibly to use the men's room. When Richie saw the car's hood go up, and the attendant's head disappear behind it, he would rifle the cash register. He was careful to ring up the identical sale already recorded on the register, and to take only clean bills, which could not be traced.

One night during a furious snowstorm Richie rang up a sale on a huge register and nothing happened. No matter how hard he banged and pried at the register drawer he couldn't budge it, so in a moment of desperation he hoisted it under his arm and carried it outside. He was almost to the car when it jerked him to a halt. He looked down and noticed a black wire leading from the register back into the station. He went back inside and unplugged it. He was halfway to Murchie's car when the attendant spotted him and began yelling "Stop Thief!" Murchie started his car and drove off with the hood still up and with Richie Connors still standing in the snowstorm holding a fifty-pound cash register and being threatened by the attendant. Richie started to run, the register cradled under his arm like a football, and the attendant, a would-be tackler, in hot pursuit. Dodging between buildings, leaping over bushes, his legs pumping and his heart pounding, Richie began to put distance between himself and his pursuer, and as he did he felt the register grow lighter and rounder and smoother and he knew for sure he'd beat his man to the goal line.

Connors was arrested the following morning. Murchie had been caught by the police the previous night and had promptly squealed. A few months later Richie was sentenced to Cheshire Reformatory, a maximum-security prison for youths under twenty-one, for a term of from eighteen months to five years. Connors still has a picture of himself as he looked on the day he was arrested. It shows a gaunt, unshaven youth with heavy-lidded eyes and sunken cheeks and a carefully combed, gleaming D.A. He was nineteen years old, 6′ tall, and weighed 162 pounds.

At Cheshire, Connors was forced to "kick" his thirty-dollar-a-day heroin habit without the aid of medicine. "Kicking cold turkey wasn't so bad," he says today. "I got chills and cramps and a fever for a few days, just like the flu, and then it was gone. It certainly wasn't like having a cartilage operation, or like they picture it in the movies. Murchie and I saw "Man with a Golden Arm" and when Frank Sinatra started screaming and beating the walls from withdrawal pains we laughed. Of course we had just shot up ourselves in the balcony so we could afford to laugh."

After fifteen months at Cheshire, Connors had gained twenty pounds, become the prison's best athlete, and earned his high school diploma. He was released on August 10, 1957, two months shy of his twenty-first birthday. He was declared a cured drug addict.

"I had been off drugs for over a year," he says, "and I knew I didn't want to go back. But I didn't know what to do. I saw no direction, no future, no college scholarship in sports, nothing for me to shoot for. I was the cock of the walk with no place to go. I got a job working construction and began playing semi-pro football again. I also had a girl friend and a new father."

After twenty years, Frances Hurley Connors had remarried. Her new husband was a chef. He did not like the idea of having a twenty-one-year-old ex-junkie living with him, and he kept hinting to Richie that he should get married and go off on his own. Finally, one night—Mothers' Day—Richie's stepfather had a heart-to-heart talk with him while his mother was at work. He told his stepson that he would be happier married, that it would be in the best interests of both Richie and his mother. After that talk he prepared an elaborate meal for the two of them.

"I went to bed thinking that everything was going to work out," says Connors. "He kept saying I was a good boy and how much everyone loved me and I fell asleep feeling fine. While I slept he started drinking alone and it must have been about 2 A.M. when he went into the bathroom and crushed about a dozen aspirins into a fine powder and put them in an envelope by my bed. Then he called the police. They arrested me at about 3 A.M. I couldn't believe what was happening. I had been clean for over a year. At the jail they said the stuff in the envelope was the purest heroin they had ever tested, and they locked me up. I stayed in prison for thirty days before they finally got a report from the Hartford laboratories that the stuff wasn't heroin. But during those days no one had believed I wasn't back on drugs. Everyone told my girl friend, 'Once a junkie, always a junkie.' Even when I was released no one believed I wasn't back on drugs.

"I got married, but things went downhill pretty fast. We argued a lot about my playing sports. My wife thought it was a waste of time, and I couldn't get her to see it was the only way I had of rationalizing my existence. When I got laid off from my construction job at Christmas I went back to drugs."

Connors devoted the next few years of his life to the pursuit of drugs, until by his twenty-fourth birthday he had a $50-a-day heroin habit. He had been arrested a dozen times, had served a number of small jail terms, and had been sent to the federal hospital for drug addicts in Lexington, Kentucky. After seven days there he was thought to be cured, and the afternoon of his release he shot up about twenty yards beyond the prison gate.

"I look back now," he says, "and see that I was almost a vegetable. I was a liar, cheat, thief, you name it. You couldn't lay ten cents in front of me that I didn't steal it. My mother used to take me by the hand to get a haircut because I couldn't be trusted with the money."

When Richie Connors was arrested for larceny in 1961, and the presiding judge noticed the number of narcotics-related arrests on his record, he declared him a thorn in the side of society and sentenced him to four years in the State Penitentiary at Wethersfield. At the time he entered prison, Richie Connors weighed 160 pounds; he had lost his teeth and his good looks from drugs; he had lost his athletic ability; and he had apparently lost even his future—all before he had reached his twenty-fifth birthday. The only thing he hadn't lost was his tremendous ego, which he had acquired partly from his mother, and partly from his participation in sports.

"It wasn't fair what was being done to me, I thought,"

says Connors today. "I was 'The Champ,' the best damned athlete in the world, even if I hadn't played sports in years. I felt if I didn't turn my life around right now I'd be an addict all my life. I'd probably end up killing some poor bastard over drugs, or maybe dying from a bad fix, or, if I was lucky, just spending the rest of my life behind bars. I was too good for that. People always said you couldn't kick junk, but I never doubted I could. I could do anything. I'd always thought I could do anything, that if I wanted to I could have been the world's greatest athlete. It became my new challenge. I would be the only guy who ever kicked heroin. It was my Super Bowl, my World Series, and it was bigger than any damned sports contest ever played because this was no imitation of life-and-death, for me it was the real thing. That thought excited me. I was fighting all the odds—my lack of weight, knowledge, maturity, attitude, past, everything—in a game that had more pressure than any athlete had ever faced and for results that were more significant than those any athlete had ever achieved. It was the thought of this competition that really motivated me."

Within ten months Connors had built his weight up to a muscular 215 pounds. He worked with weights in the prison gymnasium and began playing sports again. Soon he so excelled that he began thinking of himself as somehow different from his fellow inmates. "They were the criminals," he says. "I was here only on a mistake, a misunderstanding, which would all be straightened out soon." Even the inmates and the prison guards began to think of him as somehow apart from them. He was an athlete, not a con, they said, and so they treated him with respect. The guards made him a trusty. He was given the softest jobs, such as painting the prison's electric chair. "I used to sit in it when I was finished to see how it felt," he says. "It felt comfortable, especially since I knew I could get up and walk away from it." When his girl friend came on visiting days (he was in the process of divorcing his first wife), word spread quickly through the prison corridors, "It's Richie's girl! Tell Richie, his girl is here!"

"It was almost comical," says the present Mrs. Connors, a soft blonde who resembles Kim Novak. "I felt so conspicuous. Then Richard would come strutting into the visitors' room, his hair combed, handsome again, his khaki clothes pressed to a knifelike crease. I said to myself, 'My God, this man didn't just step out of a cell, he stepped out of Botany 500.'"

"I was doing that four years in a song," says Connors. "I had everything back, looks, weight, ability, when suddenly I realized I was still the same junkie. I still thought of myself as having been shortchanged by everyone else but me, and I knew it would take me only a few months on drugs to destroy what I had regained in prison."

Connors then began making a conscious effort at becoming introspective. He began to read, to question, and to spend more time with the most intelligent prison inmates, the lawyers and doctors and judges.

He sat with them for hours, hypnotized by the knowledge they had about themselves and the outside world. "Those guys were the best teachers a man could have," says Connors. "They had plenty of time to think out all of life's answers, only they couldn't apply them to their own lives. I took bits and pieces from rapists, embezzlers, murderers, and put my life back together again. I realized I had turned to drugs to get recognition and attention, even to the point where I became the biggest junkie and best sneak thief around. Perhaps I was afraid I might not be able to make it in sports, that I would never become a Ray Nitschke, and so I used drugs as an excuse to fail. When I got out of prison in 1965 I knew I'd never go back to drugs. That was a fact I never doubted. I also found it strange that I never again sat down to talk philosophically with people like I did with those prison cons. There was never enough time, it seemed."

When Richie Connors was finally cut from the New York Giants in 1965, his fiancée was both furious and terrified. She was furious because she felt he had been treated cruelly by the Giant players who had discovered his past. "But Richard didn't let it bother him," she said. "He said that for the next few years this was the kind of treatment he should expect. He would have to prove himself in the community first before he could expect anything better. He was very philosophical about it. That was a side of him I had never noticed before."

She was terrified for a related reason. She had been warned repeatedly by friends that she was making a terrible mistake hooking her life to that of an ex-junkie. "There is no such thing as an 'ex-junkie,' " she was told. "It'll take only one little setback to start him off again."

"The night Richard was cut," Claudette Connors recalls, "I phoned his house and he sounded so depressed. I asked him what he was going to do."

"What is there to do?" he said. "I'm going back to the same old thing."

"What do you mean?"

"Sheetrocking, what else!" he said. "I'm going back to sheetrocking tomorrow morning."

Richard William Connors, sitting at a lunch counter in the Bridgeport railroad station, looks no different from the dozens of other commuters waiting for the 7:37 A.M. to New York City. He is impeccably dressed in a double-knit blazer and double-knit slacks. He is now assistant to the president of an electrical contracting firm. An attaché case rests at his feet. His hair, still long, is no longer combed into a D.A. It falls across his forehead, modishly cut. He weighs 215 pounds. The waitress places a cup of coffee in front of him and asks if he would like a roll too.

"What kind do you have, dear?"

"Poppyseed."

Richie shakes his head. "I've been off that stuff for years," he replies, and laughs loudly.

At thirty-five years old, Connors has not touched heroin in over eleven years. When he was out of prison for only a short time he ran across Murchie and his friends one day downtown. When Murchie offered him a free bag of heroin just for starters, Connors threatened to kill him. "I was working at Herman Isaacs, a soap manufacturer," he says. "All night long we ground up dead animals into soap. I told Murchie if he ever came near me again I'd make him into a bar of Ivory."

A few years ago, Richie was visited by a friend he had known during his drug days. The friend told him of the tremendous deal he had going. He was stealing suits from a New York store and selling them all over town. "I listened to him for an hour," says Richie, "and when I came back inside I realized I hadn't understood a word he said. It was like we were talking different languages. He got arrested a short time later. I think he's serving twenty years for armed robbery or something."

Richie Connors no longer plays football either. When he was first cut from the Giants, he worked as a sheetrocker by day and a soapmaker by night. On weekends he played minor league football with such teams as the Hartford Knights, the Meriden Merchants, the Long Island Bulls, and the Bridgeport Jets, a farm team of the New York Jets. He played football for almost eight years before he finally retired. He played, he says, because it was a perfect outlet for his frustrations, but his wife claims there were other reasons.

"When Richard got cut from the Giants," she says, "it dawned on him that he might have become a major league player if it hadn't have been for drugs. After that he was obsessed with catching up to the career he had lost. He thought at thirty he could still make the pros. And secretly, I think if he could tell someone tomorrow he was only twenty-five and they'd believe him, he'd try out for the Giants again."

Today Richie Connors confines his sports activity to daily workouts at the YMCA, and to his assistant coach's duties with the Bridgeport Jets of the Atlantic Coast Football League. He paces the sidelines at those games like a caged lion, shouting orders, stabbing the air with his hands, getting so emotionally involved that often he has to be censured by referees for moving onto the playing field. For his team's final game this past season he suited up for the first time in a year and led his defensive unit with 16 tackles.

In the summer Connors is an instructor at the Offense-Defense Football Camp in Mount Snow, Vermont. The camp is attended mostly by young boys between the ages of ten and twenty who want to learn the fundamentals of football from such famous professionals as Don Maynard, Tucker Frederickson, and Joe Morrison—not to mention such less renowned players as Dick Connors. Dick Connors has been voted the camp's best coach by the students the past two summers.

But he does not attend the camp solely for the love of sport. Like some of the boys he teaches, his greatest satisfaction probably comes from rubbing elbows with such famous athletes as Maynard. Because even now—at the age of thirty-five—Richie Connors still harbors an adolescent's worship of those men who possess something he feels he has been cheated of. Connors mentions his famous acquaintances casually: "When Joe Willie and I had lunch the other day . . .", or "Wilt and I decided. . . ." He keeps a scrapbook filled with mementos of his sports past—no matter how insignificant—like a note from Joe Morrison asking Dick Connors to pick up his laundry; or a letter from the Boston Patriots advising Dick Connors that his invitation to their rookie camp had been cancelled. ("It seems they had this idea I was only twenty-five," says Richie, "and then they discovered I was really closer to thirty.") These items follow the picture of Connors as he appeared on the day of his first arrest. But now that those days are behind him, Richie Connors does not like to look at this picture. He would rather show a visitor one of the many larger-than-life photographs of himself in a Bridgeport Jets' football uniform, his hair properly tousled with sweat and his helmet cradled under his arm much in the way he once cradled that stolen cash register. Richie Connors prefers to think of himself as Dick Connors, "the former New York Giant linebacker"; that's how he introduces himself to strangers. The license plate on his used white Cadillac reads "NYG1."

There is a corner of Richie Connors' mind in which he thinks of these small liberties, these delusions of grandeur, as being proper, as being his right by ordeal. He *should* be a New York Giant; he *should* be asked for his autograph. This slightly distorted sense of his own abilities is, ironically, the very aspect of his personality that motivated him to shrug off his drug addiction. He was better than that. He was a great athlete, not a junkie. The star! This has not gone unnoticed by his acquaintances in Bridgeport, one of whom says, "Richie lives an innocent lie." Not surprisingly—indeed, with all good reason, because his home town and because this life of an innocent knows him too well—Richie Connors prefers to spend both his working and his free time in New York Cith'77urrounded by people who know him only as "Dick Connors, formerly of the New York Giants."

Yet despite his fascination with the trappings of professional sports, Richie Connors will say of himself, in moments of objective introspection, "If I'd ever become a famous athlete I'd probably be an obnoxious bastard, a guy to whom sports meant everything. I think I'm a better man for the way I used sports. Sports have meant more to me than just glory or money, although I have to admit I would like to have had those things too. Maybe I do respect famous athletes more than I should, but I don't for a moment think of them as being better than me. I've done more with sports in my life than they could ever hope to do."

Richie's past clings to him in many ways, some less significant, others more so. He carries with him such small obsessions as his desire to immediately pounce on a ringing telephone before it stops ringing. "In jail," he says, "you could always hear a phone ringing in the distance. When you're sick from withdrawal pains you're always hoping that call's from your lawyer who's got your bail money. It's an awful feeling of anxiety not knowing who is on that phone." When Richie Connors talks to someone he demands their undivided attention. He continually taps them on the arm, nudges them with his elbow, as if to make sure not only of their attention but also their physical presence. "In prison when the guards wanted to end an argument with an inmate," he says, "they just walked away from his cell. And there was no way you could get out to make him come back and listen to you. With guards, you always lost."

Today Richie Connors can walk into a strange bar and with one glance tell whether it is "a trouble place" or not. Whenever he walks a darkened street in New York he is quick to spot the revolving lights of a police car, or shadows that might conceal a mugger or two. This ability to size up touchy situations has proved more than helpful to him in his business dealings, where he must cope with men far better educated but much less instinctively aware than himself. It is this hustler's instinct he has retained over the years and put to a more positive use than in his youth. For instance, when he moonlighted as a maitre d' in a New York restaurant he noticed that the bartender liked to stay late to "close-up shop." "It was a nice humanitarian gesture on his part," says Richie. "He'd say, 'Go ahead home, Dick, I'll take care of things.' But something clicked in my head immediately, just as if I was reading a defense at the line of scrimmage." The following morning that bartender was fired for putting his hand in the till.

Yet, this hustler's instinct has also proven a disadvantage for Richie Connors. Many of his Bridgeport acquaintances think of him as a "con man." According to one, "Richie Connors thinks he's always got to have an angle, that he can never be straight with you. That kind of game gets to be boring, especially since everyone knows him. Richie's a good kid, don't get me wrong, but he wears you down, know what I mean? Jeez, you've got to admire him for what he's done with his life, but man, sometimes he can be oppressive."

Richie Connors would not deny that he lives his life with the same furious intensity as an ephemera. He would say only that, "I can't afford to relax and take my time like other people. I missed too much. For ten years I was on ice and I want to catch up. Sometimes I actually do think of myself as being only twenty-five years old, because for ten years I didn't live."

Richie moves daily at a pace and with a fury that would wilt most men. He has worked at as many as four jobs in a 24-hour span, all because of a desire to make himself both "respected" and "successful." He seems always to be moving from one place to the next, to be juggling one job for another, to be playing 1000 and 1 hands for the jackpot he feels he has missed. "I function best that way. It's exciting. It's the challenge that motivates me, the hustle, the game. Once I achieve something I get bored with it."

No matter what he is doing, whether spending time with his family (three children), or riding a train to New York, or just walking down Madison Avenue to a business appointment, Richie Connors never seems bored. He appears always to be drawing a kernel of pleasure from life's smallest parts. He stops to speak to strangers. He sings to himself. He laughs often and boisterously in a scratchy, grating voice at the smallest incident—such as the woman who almost choked on her coffee when she heard Richie say to a friend, "My number in prison? I think it was 20231. No, that was my second number. My first number was . . ."

"Richard can't stand for anyone not to be happy," says his wife. "He really does love life. I only wish he didn't love turmoil so much too. I really don't think he could live happily if things went smoothly. For instance, a few years ago I received a visit from two men who said they were from the Internal Revenue Department. I was terrified. The men said my husband hadn't filed his income tax in two years. I said I didn't know. This one man said, 'You mean you live with this man and you don't know he hasn't filed a return in two years?' I told him, 'You don't know my husband. My husband just goes along on his merry way, and all I can do is hope things work out right.' Well, I told them I wouldn't answer any more questions and they'd better talk to Richard. When they left I called him at work. I was terrified. I told him he was going to be arrested and all, and he says to me, as easy as you please, 'Don't worry dear, nothing's going to happen to me. I haven't done a thing wrong.'

" 'You haven't done a thing wrong!' I screamed. 'No, you just haven't filed your income tax form in two years, that's all! What did you do with them?'

" 'I tore them up,' he says. Can you imagine? He *tore* them up! Anyway, to make a long story short, Richard went down to the tax bureau and told those two men he was a former New York Giant player and that he had been in prison recently, and by the time he finished they made out his tax returns for him, and we got six hundred dollars back.

"To tell the truth, I can never keep up with Richard. I wish he had only one goal in life, one thing he wanted most to do. Sometimes I think he creates difficulties just so he can master them, like the drug thing, and call attention to himself. I think he has all these little plots and games because deep down inside he's afraid if he didn't, if he was just himself, people would find him lacking. But that's impossible after the things he's done with his life."

When Richie Connors hears the train, he picks up his attaché case and begins moving toward it. "I enjoy my life," he says. "I don't find too many people who deserve to enjoy it as much as I do. There aren't many things in it, now, I'd care to change. But if I felt there was one thing missing, it's that I should have become a famous athlete. I really should have made the Giants in 1965, you know." He breaks into a small trot as the train picks up speed and he is still not aboard it. Now he is running. His legs are pumping high, his attaché case is tucked under his arm. "But it's not too late," he says over his shoulder, as he grabs the railing and swings up onto the platform. "After all, I'm only twenty-five."

January 1972

From *A False Spring*

I see myself daily as I was then, framed in a photograph on the desk in my attic room. The picture was taken on June 27, 1959, at County Stadium in Milwaukee, Wisconsin, a few minutes before the Milwaukee Braves were to take the field against the Chicago Cubs, to whom they would lose that day 7–1.

I am standing midway between the firstbase line and the home team's dugout. To my back I see the stadium's half-filled bleachers. I am wearing a Braves' uniform. Although the photograph is black and white, I see all the colors. My cap has a navy crown, a white M, and a red bill. My flannel uniform is the color of cream. It is trimmed—shirt and pants—with a half-inch-wide, tri-colored stripe of black and red and black satin. The word "Braves" is scripted in red and outlined in black at a slight upward angle across the front of the shirt. The

165

script is underlined by a black and gold tomahawk. Below the tomahawk, in the left-hand corner of the shirt is "24" in large block numerals, also red and outlined in black. Unseen in the photograph but clearly in my mind's eye is the small gold patch stitched onto the shirt sleeve below my left shoulder. It is the face of an Indian of indeterminate tribe, the face contorted by a war cry no less menacing for being inaudible.

To my right is Whitlow Wyatt, the Braves' fifty-two-year-old pitching coach. Wyatt is smiling at me. My gaze, however, is directed to my left toward Warren Spahn, the Braves' great left-handed pitcher. Both Spahn and I are perspiring. We have just finished running wind sprints in the outfield and are apparently on the way to the clubhouse to change our shirts when we stop to pose for this photograph. . . . For whom? For some faceless fan leaning over the dugout roof, imploring "Please!" whose good fortune it was to catch us in an obliging mood? So we stop, strike a pose, so casual, and wait for the camera's click. To pass this moment, as he has innumerable others like it, Spahn, hands on hips, turns to me with some bit of small talk, a phrase, meaningless, meant only to fill the instant. And I listen. Nonchalantly, hands on hips also, I listen to Spahn. To Spahnie. To Spahnie who is talking to me, so much younger, and yet with my amused smile looking so at ease—today amazed at how truly at ease I do appear, at how naturally I did fit, in that uniform, between those men, with Spahn, Spahnie and I, the best of friends, I too having done this small thing so often, having struck this obliging pose for so many fans, waiting only for the camera's click before tossing off a remark at which Spahnie and I would laugh on the way into the clubhouse to change our shirts.

I was eighteen years old that day and the photograph had been arranged by the publicity department of the Milwaukee Braves, with whom I had just signed my first professional baseball contract. Of all the major league uniforms I wore that summer—and I wore many—none was so gaudy and none so impressive as the uniform of the Braves. That was one reason I signed with them rather than with one of the other 15 league teams who had also offered me a contract. There were other reasons. The Braves had agreed to pay for my college education, to pay me a salary of $500 per month during each baseball season, and to deposit in my savings account every June 27 for the next four years a certified check for $8750. All told, my bonus amounted to more than $45,000 distributed over a four-year period. It was one of the largest bonuses—if not *the* largest—any young player received from the Braves in 1959. For my part, I promised to leave Milwaukee the following morning on a flight to McCook, Nebraska, where I would begin my professional career as a pitcher with the McCook Braves of the Class D Nebraska State League.

I pitched in the minor leagues for three years, at towns like McCook, Davenport, Waycross, Eau Claire, and Palatka, before I was given my unconditional release by those same Milwaukee Braves. I never did pitch a game in Milwaukee County Stadium, nor did I ever again speak to Warren Spahn. I did, however, keep the cash.

I remember the first game I pitched that last spring, although whether it was against Jacksonville or Cedar Rapids or Yakima, I'm not sure. I remember it was still cool in March in Waycross and I had to warm up a long time in the bullpen. I remember too that I did not feel right as I threw. My motion felt awkward. I had no rhythm. There was a point in my pitching motion when all the parts of my body—throwing arm, shoulders, back, hips, legs—should have been exploding in unison toward the plate. On this day those parts were out of sync. While the rest of my body was lunging forward, my throwing arm lagged behind. It was as if my arm was reaching back, too late, to grasp something it had forgotten. When both feet were planted in my follow-through and my body's rhythm was all but spent, then my arm began moving toward the plate. I released the ball without benefit from the rhythm that had been built up by the rest of my body. It was as if I were standing flat-footed and merely flipping the ball with my arm. Even as I threw I could feel what was wrong. But my arm had a will of its own that day and I could impose nothing on it. I bounced balls in the dirt and flung them over my catcher's head. And none of those wild pitches even faintly resembled the fastballs I'd once thrown in Davenport, Iowa.

I pitched to 12 batters that day and did not retire one. After every walk and wild pitch and base hit, I cursed and glared and kicked the dirt as I'd so often done at Davenport, and then, quite to my surprise, it suddenly occurred to me that what was happening at this moment was somehow different from anything I had ever experienced before. This thought startled me, like a strange and unexpected pinch hitter. I paused a moment between pitches and tried to focus on this different thing. When I finally did recognize it all rage left me and sense of panic set in. It started as a flutter in my stomach and rose, a solid lump, to my throat. I could not swallow! For one terrifying second I thought simply of breathing, of finally catching a breath, and only when I had was my mind free to dwell on the other thing. I'd forgotten how to pitch! I had lost control over all those natural movements—arm motion, follow-through, kick—that had been merely reflex actions for so many years. I tried to remember, saw only bits and pieces, shattered fragments of a thing once whole. I sifted through the fragments, tried to fit one to another, could not remember how to make my throwing arm move in unison with my lunging body. I could not remember how I'd once delivered a baseball with a fluid and effortless motion! And even if I could remember, I somehow knew I could never transmit that knowledge to my arms and legs, my back and shoulders. The delicate wires through which that knowledge had so often been communicated were burned out, irrevocably charred, I know now, by too much energy channeled too often along a solitary and too fragile wavelength.

Terror-stricken, I looked through the homeplate screen and saw the scouts and managers sitting in their deck chairs, shaking their heads in disbelief. A cluster of ballplayers was forming around them, growing larger with each pitch as word spread from diamond to diamond. Behind them all was the rotunda—that cylindrical brick building rising high above the diamonds. On its flat roof I could see four Braves' executives—Birdie Tebbetts, John McHale, John Mullins, Roland Hemmond—pointing me out to one another. I began my motion, tried in midmotion to remember, felt my arm jerk uncontrollably toward the plate. And then I saw the ball rising over the homeplate screen, over the heads of those behind the screen, higher still, over the top of the rotunda and the heads of the men standing behind it, the men glancing up, startled, and then following the ball with their eyes until it came down on Diamond Four. For a split second everyone—players, umpires, scouts, managers, executives—stared at the ball resting on the infield dirt behind second base, and then they all looked up at the point where the ball had passed over the rotunda, and then, in unison, they turned toward me, blank on the mound. Someone laughed, and then others laughed too.

I lost it all that spring. The delicate balance I had so assiduously created at Bradenton collapsed. Just like that. One moment it was a perfectly solid-looking structure—satisfactions, potential, success, talent—and the next it was nothing but rubble. The only thing left standing was a new and impenetrable frustration.

Each game I pitched that spring was, like the first, an embarrassment. Standing on the mound, I tried to remember. The bright sun receded in the sky, grew small and distant, dissolved. Staring plateward, I saw at the end of a long, narrow tunnel, a minute fresco: batter, catcher, umpire. I began my motion, heard from a great distance the shouts and nervous shifting of my fielders, pumped, raised both hands overhead, curiously felt no exertion, was moving as if in a dream, without effort, disconnected. I raised my left leg and turned it toward third base, paused—perfectly balanced on one leg, an odd-looking bird, still and blank—and then my body moved toward the plate, and later, my arm. The ball traveled a great distance through the dark tunnel and I lost track of it. Moments later, sensing its return, I raised my glove and caught it, without feeling. I began my motion again, threw the ball, caught it, threw it, caught it, threw it. At times I was vaguely conscious of my fielders moving after it, and then, of myself moving too (always the pitcher, even in a dream) drifting toward third base, straddling the bag now, aware of a runner moving toward me. He moves in agonizing slow-motion, his features twisted, his chest heaving and, curiously suspended over his right shoulder, a sunspot—the ball! The runner and the ball are approaching very fast now, growing larger and larger, are almost upon me when, with a ferocious grunt, the runner leaps into the air, momentarily obscuring the ball. He hits the dirt—whoomph—and slides. The ball, suddenly huge before my eyes, explodes in my glove, which instinctively slaps at his spikes, too late. *"Safe!"*

Amid the billowing dust, I am conscious now of the sun's glare and my labored breathing and my hot, coarse-flannel uniform dripping sweat and the heavy ball in my hand and the nauseating, oily-leather smell of my glove and the pressing shouts and whistles of my teammates and, finally, walking back to the mound, of the weariness of my limbs.

In camp that spring I became "the bonus baby who forgot how to pitch." I took to my room and locked the door. I played my records at full volume and hid behind the noise. I no longer drove into town for a beer or dinner at Ma Carter's. I took all my meals in camp. I ate either very early, before the others filled the cafeteria, or else very late, after they had eaten and gone. I seldom left my room in barracks two. I passed the time standing for hours in front of the mirror on the wall. I practiced my motion in pantomime. I threw a thousand pitches a day in front of that mirror. At first I went through my motion as quickly as if I was pitching in a game, because I hoped to slip naturally into a once familiar groove. Then, when that did not work, I went through my motion with great deliberation, step by methodical step, looking always for that point where everything started to go wrong. But all I ever saw reflected in that mirror was my own image. It hypnotized me. In midmotion my mind would drift, and by the time I forced it back I'd be in my follow-through.

No amount of throwing before that mirror, or in games, or on a warm-up mound with old "Boom-Boom" Beck beside me extolling the virtues of the fadeaway, halted my pitching decline. It generated its own momentum and I could do nothing to stop it or even slow it down. After each game in which I performed, I slid further down through the Braves' farm system—from Austin to Jacksonville to Cedar Rapids to Yakima to Boise and, finally, to Eau Claire, Wisconsin, of the Class C Northern League. I broke camp with Eau Claire, an act of kindness by the befuddled Braves' front office.

I reached Eau Claire in late April with my wife, who had joined me at the end of spring training, after a three-day drive from the southeastern corner of Georgia to the northwestern corner of Wisconsin. The land, like Nebraska, was barren of trees, but not flat. It was rich farm and dairy country of gentle undulations that had been divided into perfect square-mile plots of corn and wheat and oats and hay and grass and freshly furrowed dirt that was almost black. From the crest of one of these undulations (not even a hill, really, just a rise) one could see a gigantic patchwork quilt of green and gold and chocolate squares, the quilt rising and falling over a softly rumpled land.

Eau Claire was a neat, nondescript little city of about

30,000 people, most of them of Swedish or German ancestry. At one end of the city was a public park built on and around a hill. The base of the hill—the park's entrance—was ringed by a narrow stream crossed by only a single bridge. Across the bridge was an open area with picnic tables, swings, seesaws and jungle gyms. Higher up the hill, the park grew thick and lush with trees and shrubs and rocky gardens. At the top of the hill, at the center of another open space, was a huge, cold, stone facade—the entrance to the city's only lighted baseball stadium and the home of the Eau Claire Braves.*

Carol and I lived in a single room with a tiny kitchen on the second floor of an old two-family house. The room was so small that once we pulled the bed out of the sofa (a Castro convertible of undecipherable vintage) it was no longer possible to cross from one side of the room to the other without walking on top of the bed. In the morning, if I woke first, I had to step carefully over my sleeping wife in order to get to the kitchen. The kitchen, which was just wide enough for two people to slip by each other, contained an ancient gas stove, a sink, some wall cabinets, two fold-up chairs and a one-by-three-foot folding table that dropped out of the wall at will.

It was there that Carol prepared the first meals of our early married life. I remember, especially, the first one.

---

* Hank Aaron began his baseball career as an eighteen-year-old second baseman with the Eau Claire Braves in the early 1950s.

She had remained at home to prepare a late supper while I went off to pitch my first game of the season. I was hurt to think she felt it of greater importance to prepare our first meal than to see me pitch, although I knew she had never been much impressed by my talent. I remembered the first time we met, in my senior year of high school. When she asked my name, I lowered my eyes and, through modestly furrowed brows, said distinctly, "Pat Jordan." Nothing! She had never heard of me! All the while we dated, I waited impatiently for the day when she would acknowledge my greatness. Why else would she be interested in me? Finally, someone told her I was a baseball star. But this did not impress her much. She knew nothing about baseball, found it amazing that someone would actually pay me a large sum of money, as she put it, "Just to play a game."

"You don't understand," I said, and dismissed her ignorance. But now in Eau Claire it disturbed me that, unlike most baseball wives, mine knew nothing about the game I devoted my life to. She took her cues solely from my enthusiasms and despairs. Whenever I pitched decently enough (a rarity that year) I had to tell her so, and only then would she smile and say, "That's nice, dear." And when I was knocked out of the box in the first inning (a more common occurrence) and she saw my dejection, she commiserated, saying, "Well, it's not your fault. It's hard to do good when you only play a little bit. . . . Why doesn't your manager let you play as long as the other pitchers?"

On the night of my first starting assignment I pitched less than an inning. It was like Waycross. After I was relieved, I had to sit on the bench in the dugout in 30-degree weather (it was always cold in the Northern League) until the game ended two hours later. When I returned to our apartment at midnight, I found the table set, dishes gleaming, napkins folded and a single candle, unlighted. Carol was sitting by the table, her hands folded in her lap, her eyes pink-rimmed. On the counter next to the stove was a mound of freshly peeled but uncooked potatoes and a long, thick, raw steak.

She sniffled, shivering all over as if just emerging from cold water. "I couldn't light the oven," she said, finally.

"What!"

She held up a pack of matches with only a single match left. "I tried, but it wouldn't catch!"

"Jesus, Carol, I'm starved!" She began to cry (the failed wife), and between sobs to plead forgiveness. Her martyred husband, returning from a hard night's work (less than an inning?) to find a barren table, decided, on a whim, not to grant it.

"If you can't cook, I'll eat someplace else," I said and turned toward the door. She clutched at my arm, caught it. "You can't leave me!" she screamed. "You can't! Please! Don't leave me alone!" Her eyes were glazed like a trapped animal's, and, for an instant, she frightened me. "I'll try again! *Please!*" She grabbed the book of matches and worked to light the last one. She struck the match over and over again, but it would not light. She stopped, finally, saying, "Please don't leave me alone," and then, exhausted, she sat down in a chair—a strange, frightened, hysterical girl . . . my wife! At nineteen! Soft and pale, with translucent skin. You could see through her, so easily . . . bluish veins and blood vessels, faint fibers in exquisite parchment.

She bruised easily, cried often that first year after she had stepped—smiling, trusting, and innocent—on board a sinking ship with its mad captain. A thousand miles from home for the first time in her life, she was burdened with nothing but my black moods day after day, while I, obsessed with my disintegrating career, seldom gave her a thought. She was just there, hovering around my despairs, at times a pleasant diversion, at other times a burden. To her, I was her husband, the sole source of comfort and despair, and she wondered, secretly, if this was the way it was supposed to be? Always?

After two disastrous performances in Eau Claire I was relegated to the bullpen. Two weeks later I was the tenth pitcher on a 10-man staff. I mopped up in the last inning of lost causes, and, even then, often had to be relieved because I could not get three outs. During the next month I appeared in six games totaling 15 innings, was credited with two losses and no victories, and had an earned run average above eight.

Only three incidents stand out in that first month. I remember pitching an inning in Duluth, Minnesota, and later being asked by a Duluth player, "Aren't you the guy from Davenport? The one who could really bring it?" I nodded, embarrassed. "What happened to you? Your motion's all fucked up." Another time, I remember pitching to Lou Brock in St. Cloud, Minnesota. At the time, Brock was leading the league in hitting with a .380 average. I struck him out on a soft, floating fastball. He swung so far ahead of the pitch that he asked the catcher if it was an off-speed pitch. At the end of the inning I sat down in the far corner of the dugout and cried. My teammates glanced over at me in disbelief. I cried uncontrollably, and my manager had to send another pitcher to the bullpen to warm up and pitch the next inning.

A third time, I remember a game in Winnipeg that began in weather so cold—19 degrees above zero—that we had to build small fires on the dirt floor of the dugout to keep our fingers from going numb. We huddled around the fires, simian man in gray flannel, and at the end of each inning sent one of our tribe to forage twigs and bits of paper in the open area behind the outfield fence. Because I was the player least likely to be used in that game, I was the one sent out to forage.

By June I no longer pitched, not even the last inning of hopelessly lost games (which were many, since the Braves were in last place). I spent each game in the bullpen. I warmed up constantly, inning after inning, trying to recapture what had once been as natural to me as walking. I became more obsessed and frantic as I threw, and my motion became even more distorted. I was pushing the ball now, like a shot-putter, and I remembered, without irony, Dennis Overby pushing the ball in spring training after his arm went bad. But there was nothing wrong with my arm! I could have understood a sore arm, dealt with it, accepted it eventually. What was happening to me was happening in my head, not my arm. Whenever I began to throw a ball, my head went absolutely blank, and afterwards it buzzed with a thousand discordant whispers.

After awhile in that Eau Claire bullpen, no one would catch me anymore, neither our third-string catcher, nor any of my fellow pitchers, all of whom thought me mad, but comically so. I threw alone, without a ball. I stood on the warm-up mound, pumped, kicked and fired an imaginary baseball toward the plate. Behind me, my teammates sat on a bench gesturing at me with their heads and laughing.

I hadn't pitched in a game for two weeks when the Braves' minor league pitching coach, Gordon Maltzberger, passed through Eau Claire. Maltzberger spent the spring in Bradenton with Milwaukee and Louisville, while Boom-Boom Beck worked with the lower minor leaguers in Waycross. During the season, however, Boom-Boom returned to his home, while Maltzberger moved up and down the Braves' minor league system, stopping a day or two in Palatka, three days in Eau Claire, five in Cedar Rapids, a week in Jacksonville and ten days in Louisville before beginning from the bottom all over again. He was a prim, fussy man in his late forties, who had pitched briefly in the major leagues during World War II. He wore horn-rimmed glasses and had thin lips always pressed so tightly together that a hundred tiny lines had formed like stitch marks around his mouth, which made him resemble a prissy, taciturn spinster.

At Eau Claire, Maltzberger spent his time giving encouragement to those pitchers pitching well and avoiding those, like myself, who were not. In the bullpen one night, I asked him to help me with my motion. "I'll get to you in good time," he said. I grabbed his forearm. "But you've got to—now!" I said. He looked down at my hand on his arm. I let go. "I'll get a catcher," I said. He did not hear me. He was still looking curiously at his arm. He shook it out away from his body, as if shaking off an insect. Then he walked back to the dugout, showered, and left that night for Cedar Rapids.

Three more days passed. My manager, Jim Fanning, had not spoken to me in a week. He passed me with a nod and quickly averted eyes. Finally I confronted him in our deserted clubhouse one night. I demanded that he pitch me. "I haven't pitched in two weeks!" I said. I could hear my shrill voice and feel the tears sliding down my cheeks. It embarrassed me. Still, I could not stop. "Everyone pitches but me! When am I gonna pitch?"

He too looked at me curiously. Then warily. His features clouded—narrow eyes, long sharp nose, lipless grin, all slanting upward toward his temples like the features of a fox. He was a trim, good-looking man in his thirties who would grow trimmer and better looking with age. By forty he would resemble one of those well-tailored gentlemen sipping an expensive Scotch in the pages of *The New Yorker*. A catcher in the Chicago Cubs' farm system, he had never risen higher than the American Association (AAA). There he was a bullpen catcher, who made good use of his idle time. He pasted newspaper photographs of prominent players in action on plywood and cut out their silhouettes. During each game, young boys hawked these mementos in the stands for one dollar.

Fanning called his business "Jim Fanning Enterprises," and, in truth, he was an enterprising man. Even at Eau Claire he had the distracted air of someone who had no intention of remaining a lowly minor league manager for very long. Sitting at the far end of the dugout during our games, he seemed always to be contemplating strategy—not for those games, but for his career. His players knew this. "Jim's gonna be a big man someday," they prophesied. "He don't belong in a uniform."

They were right. Today, Jim Fanning is the general manager of the Montreal Expos. I saw him a few years ago in the ballroom of the Lord Baltimore Hotel during the Orioles–Pirates World Series. The ballroom was filled with hundreds of baseball executives who had just finished dinner and now, over Scotches and bourbons, were proposing trades to one another. They scribbled names on paper napkins with felt-tip pens, then hurried to another table and presented the names to a rival executive. Jim Fanning sat alone at an oval table sipping from a glass and sucking on a long cigar. In his forties now, he looked impeccably trim and distinguished in a navy blazer, gray slacks, and black patent-leather loafers. While he sipped and smoked, various men came up to him, presented their napkins and waited. Jim thought for long moments, contemplated strategy while blowing smoke through puckered lips toward the ceiling, then nodded. When he was alone, finally, I went over and introduced myself.

"Remember me, Jim?" I said, standing before him. "At Eau Claire in 1961?"

He grinned at me and, without rising, shook my hand. "Sure I do, Pat. How you been?" And then, really remembering, his features began to cloud exactly as they had that night years before when I'd confronted him, hysterically, in our clubhouse. On that night he had said, "Sure you're gonna pitch, Pat. Just calm down. I was gonna start you in Winnipeg on Sunday."

We left for Winnipeg, the first stop of a thirteen-day road trip, after a Saturday night game in Eau Claire. It was midnight when we finished storing our bags in the backs of three identical station wagons (black 1958 Chevys with a screaming Indian painted on each front door) and then got inside (three players in front, three in back) and drove off toward Winnipeg, 12 hours to the northwest. Sitting by the window in the front seat, I remember watching the highway unroll before our headlights like a beckoning white-striped carpet. We drove for hours with nothing to see but the highway and the black, limitless Minnesota woods. And then, about an hour from Fargo, North Dakota, we saw a brilliant white light in the darkness, and we stopped to eat at a truckers' cafe. The cafe glowed like a star in the center of a vast open space dotted with dimly lighted gasoline pumps. The area was crowded with small-cabbed, big-bellied diesel trucks, some of them parked off in the darkness, others being gassed up at the pumps, still others hissing steam, grinding gears and roaring off down the highway.

When we finished eating and returned to the car I sat in the middle of the front seat, my knees jammed up to my chest because of the drive shaft hump, as we crossed the flat, open plains of North Dakota. Pat Sherrill drove and I sat beside him. Around us, the others slept, their heads resting on one anothers' shoulders. Whenever they woke with a start they looked around, embarrassed, and tried to go back to sleep sitting straight up. After awhile they began to list again, their heads drooping in stages, and before long they were sleeping just as before.

In the front, I could not sleep. I was too cramped in that middle seat (I could feel the muscles in my calves fluttering) and I was too excited about the prospect of finally pitching again. But most of all I could not sleep because Pat Sherrill was driving. He drove transfixed, his eyes glassy and wide and his hands gripping the steering wheel so tightly that his knuckles were bloodless. He never let the speedometer dip below 90. Whenever he saw an approaching bend in the road, the tip of his tongue would dart back and forth across his lips and he would hunch forward over the wheel in anticipation. He'd plow into that curve at 90 miles an hour, the rear end of the wagon beginning to drift, sliding as if on ice into the opposite lane while the front end pointed toward the woods and we were navigating that curve sideways, tires screeching and the stink of burning rubber everywhere. Halfway through the turn, Pat would nail the accelerator to the floor, spin the steering wheel to the left, and the rear end would snap back and the front end would straighten out and we'd roar down the highway without ever having dipped below 90.

Pat loved to drive. He refused every offer of relief on those 12-hour trips, told us he had driven with his wife and baby in a two-seat Triumph from their home in Sonora, Texas, to Eau Claire without stopping, except for gas and food and to make love to Linda in the front seat while the baby slept in the tiny compartment under the back window. That drive helped build up his stamina for his true vocation, he said, which was not to become a major league third baseman (under which assumption the Braves had given him a $20,000 bonus) but a race car driver on the NASCAR circuit. His idol was not Eddie Mathews but a wild and, then, unknown young racer also from Sonora named A. J. Foyt.

We reached Fargo at dawn. Pat turned right onto Highway 29 and we drove directly north toward Canada. We drove for hours without seeing anything but the endless gray Dakota plains and an occasional farmhouse off in the distance, and when at mid-morning we crossed the Canadian border into Manitoba Province, still the land did not change. We reached Winnipeg at noon, went directly to our hotel rooms and fell asleep, fully clothed, on the bed. I woke two hours later, stiff and malodorous, and went downstairs to the coffee shop for breakfast.

We arrived at the stadium at 3:30 P.M. for a five o'clock game. We dressed into our uniforms in the clubhouse off the left field foul line and then walked across the diamond toward our dugout along the firstbase line. The Cardinals were taking batting practice, so some of us stopped at short or second base to chat with players we had known from other leagues, other years. We would take no batting practice after our exhausting drive, only infield practice. The others broke out the bats and balls from the canvas sacks and began games of catch and pepper. I stepped down into the dugout, sat on the bench and waited (the starting pitcher's privilege) for Jim Fanning to toss me a new ball and tell me to warm up. It was a simple routine, yet one that never failed to thrill me—and certainly never so much as at that moment. The manager opens a small box, withdraws a new ball from white tissue, spits on the ball (partly for luck), rubs dirt in with the spit (the ball no longer white now, but the color of rich cream), tosses it to that day's starting pitcher and says, with a wink, "Go get 'em, Pat!"

Jim Fanning tossed me a ball and told me to go to the bullpen. "But don't warm up yet," he said. I sat in the right field bullpen and watched our team take infield practice. I grew anxious as game time drew near. Finally, one of my teammates came sprinting toward me. I stood up, flexed my shoulders, touched my toes twice. It was Hummitzsch. He tossed me a catcher's mitt. "Jim wants you to warm me up," he said. "He can't spare a catcher right now."

"But I thought . . . he told me I was starting . . ."

"I only know what he told me," Hummitzsch said, and stepped onto the mound. I caught him until he was warm, each pitch a blur through my tears. When he returned to the dugout I remained in the bullpen for a few minutes, and then I walked across the outfield to our clubhouse. I changed into my street clothes without showering, packed my blue canvas bag with "Braves" stenciled in white at both ends, and walked to the bus stop. I took a bus into town, got my other bags at the hotel and took a Greyhound bus from Winnipeg to Eau Claire.

I reached the Eau Claire bus terminal at nine o'clock in the morning and found my wife there, crying. "I didn't know what had happened to you," she said. "Everyone's looking for you. Jim Fanning called. He said you ran away. . . . I didn't know. . . . I thought

you'd left me too. . . ." She began to laugh and cry at
the same time. "I had this ridiculous vision. You were
running like a madman through Canada, you were in
your uniform. . . ."

That night John Mullins, the farm director, telephoned. He told me that for jumping the club I was
suspended without salary from the Eau Claire Braves. I
told him he was too late, that I had suspended the Eau
Claire Braves from my career.

"Don't be a smart-ass," he said. "We're reassigning
you to Palatka in the Florida State League. You get your
ass down there within two days or I'll see to it you don't
get your final bonus payment."

We left at six o'clock in the morning. I drove for 34
hours, stopping only for food and gas, but, unlike Pat
Sherrill, not to make love to my wife by the side of the
road. We did not speak for hours. Carol alternately slept
and stared out the window at the steadily changing land,
and again must have wondered what kind of man her
husband was.

I thought about my career. I thought about it when
we were driving around Chicago on the Tri-State Toll-
way and when we were driving straight south through
Indiana on a badly chewed up two-lane highway, and
when we passed through Evansville with its thousands of
roadside gas stations and, late in the afternoon, when we
turned east into Kentucky with its vast stretches of
grassland being nibbled by sleek horses. I was still think-

ing about it when we passed through Owensboro with its beautiful white-pillared mansions set far back off the road, and when we turned south again and headed toward the mountains around Nashville, Tennessee.

We reached the first mountain late at night in a dense fog. While Carol slept, I fell in behind a long trailer-truck moving slowly up the grade. The truck moved slower and slower as the mountain grew steeper and steeper, and then it was barely moving at all and the driver was shifting gears feverishly and the truck was lagging between each shift, sliding backward before the gears finally caught and it began moving forward again. I snapped alert; saw in my rear view mirror the road disappearing in the fog and off at the side of the road the mountain falling away into blackness. I was sweating now and my back ached from being held so rigidly as I leaned forward over the steering wheel. Suddenly the truck stopped, the square back end of its trailer looming huge in my windshield. I jammed on the breaks just in time. The truck then slid a few feet before stopping again. I looked in my rear view mirror; it was filled with the headlights of another trailer-truck. The truck in front exhaled a blast of smoke, lurched forward and disappeared. I released the brakes, pressed the accelerator pedal too hard and my rear wheels began to spin. Then they caught and the big Chrysler leapt over the top of the mountain and went speeding down the other side. I stabbed at the brakes repeatedly, but the mountain was so steep that we continued to hurtle down into the fog amidst the smell of burning brake linings.

I was still thinking about my career when we reached Chattanooga at dawn and a little later when we crossed into Georgia, the land of red clay. Carol, who'd been sleeping against the door, lifted her head and mumbled, "Where did we stop last? What state is it?" and then fell back to sleep before I could answer. She was still sleeping when I drove around the outskirts of Atlanta with its glass skyscrapers in the distance and, up close, the unpainted wooden shacks of the Negro slums. She did not wake until mid-morning, when we were deep into the South of two-lane black-tops and fetid swamps and a white-hot sun and lone Negroes walking along the soft, sloping shoulder beside the road. One of those black figures waved to us as we whooshed past. I beeped the horn, too late.

On the outskirts of Cordele we stopped at a fruit stand and bought six peaches for breakfast. We ate the peaches as we drove toward Tifton. The juice dribbled down our chins and onto our clothes, but we did not care. We did not care that our breath was sour and our bodies rank with sweat and that our clothes stuck to our skin. We were inured to every sensation, to aching backs and cramped limbs and burning eyes. After 30 hours of driving nothing mattered but that we finally arrive. Carol did not even seem to notice (or, if she did, she no longer cared) that the Chrysler was hurtling along at over 110 miles an hour and that I was driving with one arm out the window and only one hand on the steering wheel.

We passed through Valdosta at noon, crossed the Florida state line, and headed south toward Lake City, which we reached an hour later, and then turned southeast toward Lulu and Guilford and Lake Butler and Starke, where we saw a sign, "Palatka 39 miles." I was still thinking about my career. I had been thinking about it for 33 hours and I still did not understand it, what had happened to it, to me. As we approached Palatka, I decided that nothing had happened, nothing momentous, that is, nothing that would not be straightened out once I began pitching regularly again. That was all there was to it, I told myself, although I knew that the Braves did not share this belief. Why else would they have sent me to "The Elephants' Burial Ground?" That's what we jokingly called Palatka during spring training. It was the lowest of the Braves' Class D teams, a receptacle for aging veterans playing one last season; for all those faceless "Lefties" and "Studs" who were used to fill out a roster until midseason, when they were released; and for one-time prospects trying to make it back from calcium deposits and ripped tendons; and for others, like myself, who had somehow missed it along the way for a reason that was, as yet, unclear to anyone.

I lived in Palatka with Carol for eight weeks, and I remember it with almost the same clarity of detail I do

McCook—although for a different reason. Palatka was the last place where I played professional baseball. It was different from McCook. McCook was stark, desolate, exposed, surrounded by limitless horizons that left one breathless. Palatka, resting on the banks of the St. Johns River, was surrounded by dense tropical foliage, the limitless swamps and, overhead, a pitiless sun that smothered one's breath. It was always hot in Palatka, and it rained daily. The land never dried. All the wooden buildings rested on cinder blocks a foot off the ground, and yet even that did not prevent the moisture and the heat and the insects from eating away the wood. Warm, moist pieces of wood came off in one's hand, so that it seemed one could peel away the walls of a building like an orange if he wished to. The town's main street was called Lemon Street. It was made of cobblestones. Weeds grew between the stones and out of the cracks in the sidewalks and at the bases of the concrete buildings, so that the vegetation appeared to be strangling the town as the swamp on the outskirts crept relentlessly in. There was a paper mill that supplied most of the blacks and poor whites with employment. Each morning at six o'clock they were summoned to work by the blast of a shrill whistle that woke the entire town. Shortly thereafter the town was blanketed by a lavender haze and a terrible stench that lifted only slightly at night when the mill shut down.

Palatka was a suffocating place, claustrophic, and everything in it emitted an overwhelming sense of decay.

We came in on Lemon Street and drove slowly over the cobblestones past Pig's Bar-B-Q and the Wyn Dixie Supermarket and the old Howell Movie Theater, featuring Judy Holliday in *The Solid Gold Cadillac*. We stared out the windows at our new home and, in turn, were regarded by the townspeople. Mostly aged, they sat on benches that lined both sidewalks and faced the street. We passed through their gaze as through a gauntlet and came on an unbelievably pure chalk-white building— the pool hall. The sidewalk beside the pool hall was splattered with white too, as if both had been doused liberally with all the leftover talcum powder its customers had rubbed on their hands. We stopped before the St. James Hotel, the tallest building in town. In the lobby, old men dozed in faded armchairs, while overhead a huge fan churned so slowly I could count its blades. We registered with the grinning clerk. He wiped a handkerchief across his brow. "Hot 'nuff for y'all?" he said.

Fully clothed, we fell asleep on an old iron poster bed and did not wake from this, the longest of all road trips, until the following night. We then ate spareribs at Pig's and drove out to the ball park to watch my new teammates play. They were not called the Braves, I learned from the hotel clerk, but the Azaleas. "After the town flower," the clerk said. "They play their games in 'The Bowl'," he added with a touch of pride. "The Azalea Bowl." A slightly pretentious name for a Class D ball park, I thought, until we arrived there and I saw the name was not so much pretentious as it was ludicrous. The Azalea Bowl was similar to McCook's Cibola Stadium, except that Cibola, a speck on the plains, was a temporary, skeletal structure that looked as if it had been assembled yesterday from a few planks and metal braces and could just as quickly be disassembled tomorrow without leaving a trace. "The Bowl" (as the players leeringly called it) was a slightly more permanent looking structure at the edge of a swamp. It was enclosed by a 10-foot high fence that began behind the left field bleachers, went behind the homeplate stands, and terminated behind the right field bleachers. The fence had been painted green years ago, but the paint had mostly peeled away and now the wood had begun to rot. The outfield was enclosed by a three-foot fence whose purpose seemed less to define home runs than to hold back the swamp. Thick green foliage hung over the wall, obscuring the faded names of restaurants and gas stations that had been advertised there. Long vines and tendrils crept under the wall onto the playing surface, so that often, when an outfielder chased a ball to the wall, those perverse vines would tangle in his spikes and trip him up. Each week it seemed the vines crept further onto the playing field and the swamp pressed closer, overrunning The Bowl just as it was overrunning the town.

Carol and I arrived at The Bowl in the third inning of a game between the Azaleas and the Tampa Smokers. We sat on the top row of the homeplate stands, which were only ten rows high. It was a tiny ball park that seated less than 1000 people. On this humid night in July, however, there were no more than 100, most of them blacks laughing and cheering in the segregated bleachers along the left field foul line.

On the field, my new teammates trailed the Smokers 4–0, under dim lights and with the noise of the swamp as a backdrop (thrashings in the foliage and the caws of strange birds). In the fifth inning, with the Azaleas trailing 7–0, a snake slithered under the outfield fence and the umpires called "Time!" while our rightfielder beat it to death with a bat. By the seventh inning the Azaleas trailed 11–0, and the moisture from the swamp had crept into the outfield in the form of a low-lying gray mist. The outfielders, concealed from the waist down, waded eerily through the mist after fly balls.

The Azaleas eventually lost that game, and were, I discovered, one of the worst minor league teams ever assembled. They had assumed last place early in the season, only to bury themselves ever deeper into the cellar as the season progressed. Their fortunes had so turned against them by the time I appeared in July that players often refused to take the field. The team's leading pitcher, "Birdlegs" Perez, a Dominican Republic dandy with a cherubic face and a body like a stick figure, had lost seven games in a row. He refused to pitch anymore. He claimed he had calcium deposits in his elbow—the occupational hazard, he protested, of delivering a 1000 different pitches (knuckleball, palmball, spitball, etc.) from a 1000 different angles (overhand, sidearm, semi-sidearm, etc.), none of which, it seemed to an impartial observer, were particularly effective.

The Azalea's leading home run hitter was Paul Cato, a portly, unshaven first baseman who looked like a sinister adversary of Eliot Ness. Paul refused to take the field one day after he'd placed his first baseman's glove beside the dugout, taken a lap around the park to loosen up, and returned to the dugout to find his glove stolen. "Enough is enough!" he was heard to shout before retiring to the clubhouse, where he sulked for the entire game.

The Azaleas' leftfielder, Tim Strickland, had been a teammate of mine at McCook. Tim was the shy North Carolinian who shook hands like an Italian film star and whose only spoken words all season were to the umpire: "You gook, you couldn't call a donkey fight!" After indifferent successes at McCook and the following year at Wellsville, Tim had become a star in Palatka. When I arrived in July he was leading the Florida State League in hitting, only a few percentage points ahead of Tampa's hustling second baseman, Pete Rose. Tim was not used to the pressure, and each day he grew more twitchy as Rose irrevocably narrowed the gap between them. He pleaded with his manager to drop his name from the starting lineup. He complained of mysterious ailments, clutching his stomach in pain or cradling his splitting head, and he accused Pete Rose of voodoo.

Finally, I heard that he cracked. He did not show up

for a Saturday afternoon game at The Bowl. Evidently—according to reports—he wandered up and down Lemon Street muttering to himself. He accosted strange women, clutched their arms, and rolled his eyes. They pulled free and hurried away. He invaded a dress shop, told a salesgirl he loved her, followed her behind a rack of summer creations. They tussled, the rack tottered, dresses spilled over a customer. She flailed at them and screamed. Tim fled to his single room on the top floor of the St. James Hotel. He sat by the window and drank a case of warm beer. He drained each bottle in a single gulp and then tossed it out the window at a passing car. Bottles exploded on car roofs, scattered across the cobblestones. Someone telephoned the sheriff. *The town was under siege!* Tim was arrested. He went meekly, sat in a cell while the sheriff telephoned the Milwaukee Braves. A decision was made. Tim was escorted to the bus depot and put on a Greyhound heading north. That was the last we ever saw of him. Later, someone reported that he was in jail—an Army stockade, actually. He was a draft dodger, they said. He finished second in the FSL batting race. There was an asterisk after his name.

Louie Haas was our second baseman. He was a courtly twenty-year-old native of Paducah, Kentucky, who had been given a $40,000 bonus three years ago and ever since had had difficulty compiling a batting average as substantial as his weight. He weighed 137 pounds. He was five feet, four inches tall and had the large brown eyes and hairless cheeks of a prepubescent boy. He dreaded every game at The Bowl. The fans berated him viciously—as they did all the Azaleas, I was to discover. We served a cathartic purpose in the lives of those fans. Our lives, at the time, were even more despairing than their own, our failures each night more ludicrous and open to derision. The fans laughed and jeered at our inadequacies, which somehow (in their eyes) diminished their own, made their drab lives seem a little less drab. Even the blacks in the left field stands laughed at the Azaleas, the niggers' "niggers."

But the fans were most vindictive with little Louie. They resented his large bonus, which, even to the most inexpert eye, seemed unwarranted by any talent he exhibited on the diamond. Mostly, though, they just felt he was the least threatening of all the Azaleas and so the safest to heap their abuse on. Unlike Cato, for instance, who glared ominously at any fan who dared criticize his cloddish footwork around first base. They questioned his manhood, accused him of lacking pubic hair, genitalia, until one night Louie could stand it no longer. A group of about four "good ole Southern boys" were sitting behind our firstbase dugout, jeering Louie's every move. They passed a paper bag back and forth, tilting their heads each time to drink from it. In the seventh inning Louie fielded a ground ball and, without a glance, fired it over Cato's head, over our dugout, into the midst of his hecklers. They dove for cover—the paper bag hanging in midair for an instant before it shattered on the stands. The ball ricocheted around the bleachers, barely missing the hecklers, then bounced onto the playing field. Louie picked it up, wiped imaginary sweat from his hand, and shook his head.

When the last out was recorded in that first night's game, Carol and I remained seated while the few fans exited and the lights were clicked off. For a moment we sat there in total darkness. "My God!" I finally said. "It's gonna be a long two months." She nodded and then got up and returned to our car in the parking lot. I went to the Azaleas' clubhouse to introduce myself to the manager burdened with this corsage of withered talent. Myself included?

His name was Mike Fandozzi. He was a thirty-six-year-old minor league veteran who had toiled for most of 18 seasons in towns like Wellsville, Boise, Yakima, and Palatka. He resembled a diminutive Victor Mature. He had slick black hair, oily skin, and a toothy smile that seemed even wider than his face. He was only five-feet, six inches tall, but he had the pronounced slouch of a seven-footer with a height complex. He was quick to smile or frown, and his winks, twitches and involuntary gestures were brought on, no doubt, by the play of the Azaleas. This was his first season as a manager (he also played the infield on occasion), and he feared that if things continued this way, it would probably be his last. Even while one talked to him he would dart furtive glances over his shoulder as if anticipating approaching doom or maybe just the hand of a Milwaukee executive, who would consign him permanently to his winter home in upstate New York where, during the off-season, his wife taught school and Mike played nineball and eightball and collected welfare checks. ("And what kind of employment are you suited for, Mr. Fandozzi?" says the caseworker, leafing through his list of jobs. Mike looks out the window at the falling snow, smiles his Victor Mature smile and says, "Mostly shortstop. But I can play a little second base, maybe third too.")

I met Mike as he was stepping out of the shower. I introduced myself and extended my hand. He looked at it for a moment and then at me. "I know about you," he said. "I know what happened at Eau Claire. I don't want none of that shit here, you understand?"

"Sure," I said. "Don't worry. All I want to do is start pitching again."

"Okay," he said. "So long as we understand each other." He smiled brilliantly and stuck out his dripping hand.

"When am I gonna pitch?" I asked. He snatched his hand back.

"See! See! That's what I mean! I'll decide that. You just keep your nose clean and be here every afternoon at 5:30. I'll handle the rest."

I nodded. He smiled again and stuck out his hand.

I was on the inactive list for two weeks. I arrived at the ball park each day at 5:30, dressed into my uniform, pitched batting practice, ran ten half-hearted wind sprints, showered, dressed back into my street clothes and joined Carol in the homeplate stands. We watched about five innings of each game, or until we were sure Mike had noticed me, and then we snuck off to Pig's for supper and then back to our apartment where we watched television and made love.

The two weeks passed slowly. I played pool in the mornings, drank lemon cokes on the benches that lined Lemon Street, then went fishing in the afternoon with Ron Pavia, the only other married Azalea besides Fandozzi and myself. Ron was a short, chunky, swarthy Portuguese from Cranston, Rhode Island, who so resembled a character in the cartoon strip "Yogi Bear" that we nicknamed him "Boo Bear." "Boo" and I went fishing every afternoon, although we never caught anything. We went first to a bait store where we bought 30 shrimp frozen in a pail of crushed ice, and then we went to a grocery store and bought six lemons and a package of Dixie cups and a few six-packs of Seven-Up, and then we went to a liquor store and bought a gallon of port wine, which we stuck in the pail with the shrimp. Finally we drove to the outskirts of town where the road passed over the narrowest part of the St. Johns River without benefit of a bridge railing. There we parked the car on a soft shoulder and sat on the edge of the road with our feet dangling over the river. We baited our hooks with shrimp and tossed them into the water, then poured some port wine over crushed ice, added a dash of Seven-Up, a squeeze of lemon, and relaxed. It was always hot in the afternoon, so hot we could look down the road and see the black tar shimmering like liquid glass. To combat the heat we refreshed ourselves often with wine coolers. Soon we no longer noticed the heat, the sweat pouring down our necks, our heads nodding on our chests, the bamboo poles now weightless in our arms gone numb. Nor did we notice that we never got a nibble, that we never saw a fish, that after awhile we had even polished off our bait along with our wine coolers.

We fished like this daily, and we probably would have continued until the end of the season if not for an experience we had late one afternoon after we had finished the last of the wine. The sun was beginning to set and it had grown dark and cool, although by then we were too stiff even to notice. We had not moved a muscle in minutes, it seemed, when suddenly there was a splash and we saw, rising straight out of the water, twisting like a corkscrew as it rose, a huge ugly fish. It had hide like rusted armor and a mean, long-billed face like an alligator's. The fish kept rising and rising in slow motion, endlessly it seemed, until it had reached a height of almost six feet and its beady pop eyes were level with our own. We stared at it, Ron and I looking into the pop eyes of the garfish and he in turn scrutinizing us with a narrow squint. Then he opened his long-billed mouth, revealing rows of tiny thumbtack-like teeth and, with a single swipe, severed both lines before slipping silently back into the river.

We said nothing. We just sat there, holding the poles

with our severed lines that no longer reached the water and staring at that point in space from which the garfish had just stared at us. Shortly thereafter we got up to leave. We threw the rest of the shrimp into the river, and then we threw the pail of ice in too, and the empty bottles of Seven-Up and wine, and then, as an after-thought, we threw in our bamboo poles. We never dared mention what we had seen—what we thought we had seen—to anyone, not even to ourselves.

I was finally put on the Azaleas' active list toward the end of July, and a few days later I won my first game of the season. I pitched five innings against the Daytona White Sox before Mike had to relieve me with the tying runs on base. My relief pitcher retired the side and then pitched three more scoreless innings to preserve my first victory in almost three months. Nothing had changed in my pitching, really. I had given up three runs on ten walks, three hits and a wild pitch. I had struck out one batter. My motion was still a disaster, and my fastball and curveball were faint shadows of what they had once been. But I had had luck that night for one thing (now that I no longer needed it), and for another, I had begun to cease to care. It relaxed me. I no longer struggled to remember. I threw easily, without thought or anxiety over my lost promise. It was hard to be tormented by one's own lost promise at Palatka, where one was surrounded by so much lost promise. We laughed at each other's inadequacies.

One night Boo Bear, playing third base, kicked two

routine ground balls into the thirdbase stands. When he returned to the dugout at the end of the inning, he sat at the far end of the bench, shaking his head in despair. Someone called down to him, "Atta boy, Boo, great hands!" Then laughed. We all began to laugh. Boo glanced sideways at his laughing teammates, his face dark and threatening, and then not so threatening, and then he was laughing too. "Ah, fuck it!"

I laughed at myself also. For the first time. After my victory over the White Sox, Louie Haas shook my hand. "Nice motion you got there, fella. Smooth, really smooth."

"Just a little something I picked up along the way," I said, and we both laughed. Ironically, I was the most successful pitcher on the club during the last few weeks of the season. I started every fourth game and often relieved between starts. In one seven-day span I appeared in four games totaling 23 innings, and I won two of them. When we left for Tampa on the last road trip of the season, I had a 4–4 record and was one of the few pitchers on the club with a .500 winning percentage. Despite such modest success, however, I was not fooled into thinking I had recaptured anything. I knew I was not throwing well, was getting by on luck, a little know-how, and indifference. I realized that my pitching had deteriorated as much as it possibly could have at Eau Claire, and now, at Palatka, I was not making progress, I just wasn't getting any worse.

I thought about all these things as we drove toward

Tampa on that hot afternoon near the end of the season. I wondered where I'd lost it, tried to discover that point where it all started going downhill. But it was like trying to read isolated, disconnected points on a graph (my argument with Torre, changing my motion in Bradenton, my nature), none of which, alone, indicated a direction. My inability to see it clearly was frustrating. I put it out of my mind, turned to Boo Bear beside me in the front seat. "Pour me one of those, Boo."

Ron had set up a small bar on the dashboard—wine, ice, Seven-Up, lemons—and he had already poured himself two coolers while I was daydreaming about lost promise.

"Aren't you pitching tonight?" he asked.

"Fuck it," I said, and he laughed. Boo poured me a drink, and a little later he poured me another, and then another and he kept on pouring until we reached Tampa, five hours later.

I started that game without a care in the world, and it didn't bother me a bit when I walked the first four batters, or when Mike came out to the mound to relieve me from the last game of my career, or when I walked into the dugout with an idiot's grin and my teammates burst out laughing.

I sobered up on the ride home that night, and wasn't grinning when we reached Palatka at four o'clock in the morning. I drove to our house and woke Carol.

"What's the matter?"

"Nothing," I said. "We're going home. Pack our things."

"But the season isn't over yet," she said. "You still have two more games."

"Don't worry," I said. "It's all right." We loaded the Chrysler with all our belongings and then, because we still owed a month's rent on our apartment, I coasted the car down the hill past our landlord's house. And then I turned the key and we drove off.

We reached Jacksonville at dawn and Brunswick a little while later, and then Savannah and Florence and Fayetteville. The towns and the time passed rapidly as I daydreamed about my career.

When we reached the city limits of Rocky Mount, North Carolina, it was dark again. We moved slowly through traffic, past motels and gas stations and traffic lights, and suddenly it occurred to me, with a chill, that I had no career. What would I be without baseball? I could think of nothing. I stopped at a red light, an interminable red light. And it was then, for the first time, that I began to wonder . . . why?

July 1974